IMAGES
of America

LAKE MINNETONKA

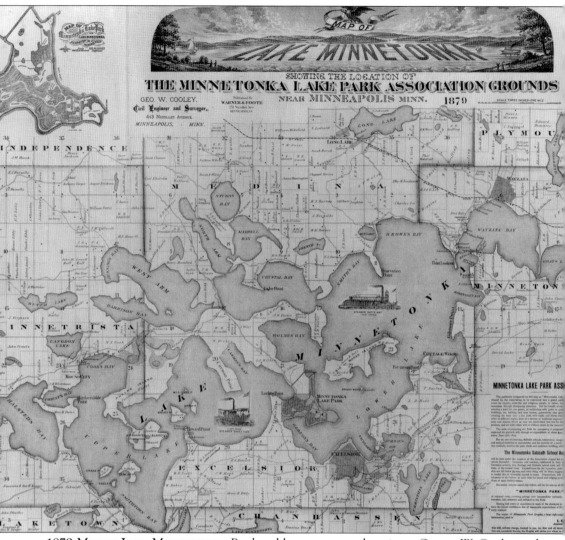

1879 MAP OF LAKE MINNETONKA. Produced by surveyor and engineer George W. Cooley and published by Warner and Foote, this map shows the entire lake area, including many property owners' names. It also details and promotes the Minnetonka Lake Park Association grounds, where the Lake Park Hotel was located. (Courtesy of the Westonka Historical Society.)

ON THE COVER: CHAPMAN HOUSE DOCKS, MOUND, C. 1896. Tourists gather around many of the lake's various watercraft—sailboats, rowboats, and the steamers *Mabel Lane*, *Helena*, and *Acte*. This photograph was taken by Charles Zimmerman, who owned Bowlder Lodge on Enchanted Island, operated a fleet of steamers, and was a noted photographer with a studio in St. Paul, Minnesota. (Courtesy of the Excelsior–Lake Minnetonka Historical Society.)

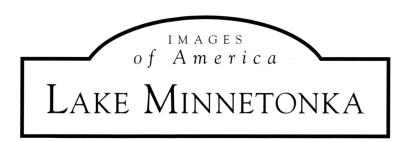

IMAGES
of America

LAKE MINNETONKA

Excelsior–Lake Minnetonka Historical Society,
Wayzata Historical Society,
and Westonka Historical Society

ARCADIA
PUBLISHING

Copyright © 2015 by Excelsior–Lake Minnetonka, Wayzata, and Westonka Historical Societies
ISBN 978-1-4671-1334-2

Published by Arcadia Publishing
Charleston, South Carolina

Printed in the United States of America

Library of Congress Control Number: 2015930411

For all general information, please contact Arcadia Publishing:
Telephone 843-853-2070
Fax 843-853-0044
E-mail sales@arcadiapublishing.com
For customer service and orders:
Toll-Free 1-888-313-2665

Visit us on the Internet at www.arcadiapublishing.com

CONTENTS

ABOUT THE AUTHORS

JOANIE HOLST. Joanie grew up on Lake Minnetonka and has been volunteering for the Wayzata Historical Society for many years. She can be found presenting programs on local history, researching in the archives, and contributing to the society's newsletter. Currently, she is the president of the organization.

LISA STEVENS. Lisa has served on the board and volunteered with the Excelsior–Lake Minnetonka Historical Society for many years. She has worked on several publications for the society, including *Walking the Trails of History*.

ELIZABETH VANDAM. Elizabeth is the treasurer for the Westonka Historical Society and History Museum in Mound, Minnesota, and contributes to the society's newsletter. She is the author of *The Doors of Tangletown, A Historical Reflection of Washburn Park* (2002), and *Harry Wild Jones, American Architect* (2008), winner of the 2009 Benjamin Franklin Silver Book Award sponsored by the Independent Book Publishers Association.

ACKNOWLEDGMENTS

This book represents the first collaboration of the Excelsior–Lake Minnetonka Historical Society, the Wayzata Historical Society, and the Westonka Historical Society. These societies have used their extensive photographic and archival collections and have consulted many Lake Minnetonka historical organizations, historians, and primary sources to provide the most accurate portrait possible of lake history. The book's scope is limited to the high-quality images of the lake area that are available, mainly from the 1860s to the 1950s, and includes images and information that are being published for the first time.

The authors wish to thank everyone who has donated, collected, and written history about Lake Minnetonka, particularly the following individuals and organizations who have been generous with their knowledge, image collections, and time: Mary Lou Bennis, Andy Bond, Doug Complin, Susanne Egli, Marty Gilbert, Drue Gisvold, Jeffrey Hatcher, Holly Holmes, Brian Holst, Bill Jepson, Susan Larson-Fleming, Paul Maravelas, Lori McCune, Mary McKenzie, Jon Monson, Pam Myers, Mary Opheim, Tom Rockvam, Dean Salita, Ginny Shafer, Sue Sorrentino, Don Stolz, Barbara Sykora, and Gerry Vandam. The authors would also like to thank everyone we have worked with at Arcadia Publishing for their guidance, patience, and support.

The authors would especially like to thank historian Scott D. McGinnis for countless hours of research, advice, support, and for generously sharing his collections and encyclopedic knowledge of Lake Minnetonka history.

The images in this volume appear courtesy of the Cottagewood General Store (CGS), Deanne Gray Straka (DGS), Excelsior–Lake Minnetonka Historical Society (ELMHS), the Elizabeth Vandam Private Collection (EV), the Hennepin County Library Minneapolis Collection (HCL), the Hennepin History Museum (HHM), Lori McCune (LM), the Minnetonka Historical Society (MTHS), Scott D. McGinnis (SDM), St. Martins-by-the-Lake Episcopal Church (SML), Tom Rockvam (TR), the Walden Collection (WC), the Westonka Historical Society (WTHS), and the Wayzata Historical Society (WZHS).

INTRODUCTION

Lake Minnetonka has always meant many things to many people. Today, we know that the lake located in western Hennepin County, Minnesota, covers 14,000 acres, with 121 miles of shoreline and a maximum depth of 113 feet. Geologists call it an ice block or kettle lake, created by melted blocks of ice from the retreating Wisconsin Glacier. The lake is fed by way of Six Mile Creek and Halsted Bay and flows out at Grays Bay into Minnehaha Creek, traveling 22 miles east to the Mississippi River.

Centuries ago, indigenous people camped here and built sacred mounds on the lake's shores. The Mdewakanton Dakota, who hunted and fished the area for many years, were said to have kept their knowledge of the lake to themselves. Soldier Joseph Brown heard the Indians speak about a large body of water "towards the setting sun, in the big woods." In 1822, he set out to find it with William Snelling and two others from Fort St. Anthony. They traveled west, following Minnehaha Creek, and came to today's Grays Bay. Upon their return, their discovery was met with disinterest. The lake remained undisturbed until the land opened for settlement following the Treaty of Mendota in 1851. History has it that when Gov. Alexander Ramsey visited the lake in 1852 and was told that the Dakota called it "Minnetonka," meaning "large water," he made the name official. Soon, newspapers proclaimed, "Perhaps no place in Minnesota is attracting more attention at present than Minnetonka."

Before photography came to the lake, its vistas were preserved with words. For the excited speculator, the pioneer filled with wanderlust, and the family anxious to learn about their future home, letters and newspaper reports were their only resource.

In 1852, John H. Stevens, one of the first settlers in what is now Minneapolis, wrote to George Bertram of the Excelsior Pioneer Association in New York:

> This is a healthy country: we have no bilious fevers . . . and cases of consumption . . . are seldom known here at all. Next, our climate, in the summer, spring, and fall, is delightful. The beautiful autumn excels any part of the year, yet our winters are cold but pleasant, the sun shines nearly every day during the whole winter months, and while it is very cold, the atmosphere is so clear and healthy that persons do not feel the cold half as much as in Missouri. Yet the mercury often freezes. I have often travelled all day long when this was so, and not felt the cold, and I was as comfortable as in mid summer, in fact, the winters are not objectionable. Now for Minnetonka: Maple sugar can be made, enough to sweeten a colony of fifty thousand souls. . . . The wild game of the country is abundant enough to support any quantity of families and as the Indians recede the game will increase. . . . Any family can procure enough fish to last them year round. . . . In winter, we are about fourteen days from New York, in summer, half that time. Not wishing you to locate here against your will, because we know of plenty who wish and are now looking for suitable places to make a permanent home. I would advise you, if you want to secure the cream of the land or the lake, to see to it this fall.

Hezekiah Brake, one of Bertram's association members, arrived soon after and wrote, "We were greatly pleased with our new home. There were no enormous rents as in the East, and we had laid in a stock of provisions that lasted some time. The Lake abounded in fish and in the forest any amount of game could be had for the shooting. Hunger is always a good sauce, but our appetites here were truly voracious."

In 1853, Brake was marooned on Big Island during an icy spring storm and wrote with a more uncertain tone, "There were noises of all sorts about us. Besides the roaring waters, wolves howled, and the woods seemed full of sounds; as I sat smoking by the blazing fire, brooding over our danger, and my wife's fears for my safety, I wished most heartily that I had never undertaken the life of a pioneer."

Indeed, Brake's wife, Charlotte, pleaded with him to leave: "When will these uncertainties, anxieties and forebodings cease? It is hastening me into insanity. Do let us leave this terrible lake country, and put an end to this interminable trouble and worry."

Brake granted his wife's wish in 1858; years later, he wrote, "My work as a pioneer was not in vain. When I landed on the lakeshore, the surrounding region was a wilderness. . . . Wild beasts infested the forest and civilization seemed far off. Now the country was being transformed into a fertile farming community. . . . Excelsior, a thriving village now stood. A church, schoolhouse, hotel, dry goods and merchandise stores, and a post office were here, and fifty-five persons might be counted as residents."

This same story could be told of many of the settlements around the lake. George Day remembered, "Pioneer days with scattered populations of honest, whole-souled, hard-working settlers, who, notwithstanding the fact that they were held in the grip of poverty and privation, left the latch-string of their humble doors always hanging out; and the man looking for a claim, or a family moving in, was always welcome; for no cabin was too small to shelter the strangers."

As photographers arrived at the lake, a new record of its beauty, settlement, and everyday life was created. Representing over a century of preserved history, the images in this book bring clarity to the way we perceive the lake's past and shape its future.

One

HOMESTEADS AND
NAMESAKES

By 1855, all of the Lake Minnetonka shoreline was claimed. Many of the settlers were well educated Easterners seeking adventure, and word spread quickly about the desirability of the lake area. The first Lake Minnetonka settlement in Minnetonka Mills was founded by Simon Stevens and millwright Calvin Tuttle in 1852. Sawmills turned the woods into the towns of Excelsior, Minnetrista, and Wayzata. Excelsior, meaning "ever upward," was founded by New Yorker George Bertram and his Excelsior Pioneer Association in 1853. Wayzata was platted by Oscar Garrison and Alfred Robinson in 1854. As the northernmost community on the lake, its name is commonly translated to mean "north shore" in the Dakota language. At the extreme southwest, known as the Upper Lake, German Home Township was established in 1858 and renamed Minnetrista one year later. In 1876, the village along Cooks Bay was named Mound City for the abundance of earthen mounds surrounding the area, said to be the work of prehistoric inhabitants.

Today, the names given to area bays, points, roads, and islands recall early families. To the north, Stubbs Bay is named for this Orono farming family, while tiny Gale Island was first called Gooseberry Island before Harlow Gale purchased it in 1872 for under $4. Gideon Bay was named for the enlightened and tenacious Peter Gideon, a staunch abolitionist and horticulturist ahead of his time. On the Upper Lake, William Noble bought the largest island on the lake, which he sold to Carrington Phelps in 1875, now Phelps Island.

Lake Minnetonka homes reflect varied economic backgrounds, from seasonal cabins with basic amenities to year-round residences of all sizes. The summer homes and boathouses of the wealthy punctuated the shoreline among the cottages, hotels, and farmhouses, prompting the *Minneapolis Tribune* to remark in 1892, "Cottage architecture will one day become its [the lake's] most famous feature." By 1950, few estates were still intact, becoming residential subdivisions. Some, like Chimo and Walden in Deephaven, and Belford in Wayzata, remain private residences.

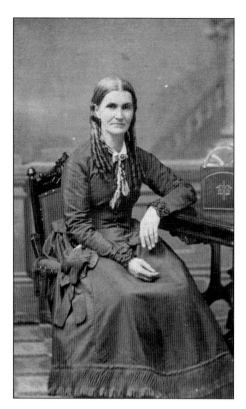

SARAH CHOWEN SHAVER, 1876. In 1852, Sarah Shaver, her husband, James, and son Eldridge were the first settler family in the lake area. James was a carpenter at Minnetonka Mills, and Sarah cooked for the crew. In 1853, they moved to their claim south of Wayzata Bay, and Sarah gave birth to twin boys, the first children born to settlers in the area. She died in 1884 and is buried in Minnetonka's Groveland Cemetery. (ELMHS.)

REV. CHARLES GALPIN. Among the first to arrive in the Excelsior area, Galpin founded the Independent Church of Excelsior and Chanhassen in 1853, the Excelsior Institute in 1857, and the Excelsior Academy in 1885. After leaving the ministry in 1855, he worked as a dentist and operated the first steamboat on Lake Minnetonka, the *Governor Ramsey*, delivering mail and shuttling travelers. Galpin Lake is named for him, and he is buried in Excelsior's Oak Hill Cemetery. (ELMHS.)

GEORGE BERTRAM. A tailor from New York City, Bertram explored Lake Minnetonka in 1852 and founded the Excelsior Pioneer Association. Returning to New York, he sold shares to association members, entitling them to a farm and village lot. In 1853, members settled in Excelsior, but Bertram moved to Wright County, Minnesota, several years later. (ELMHS.)

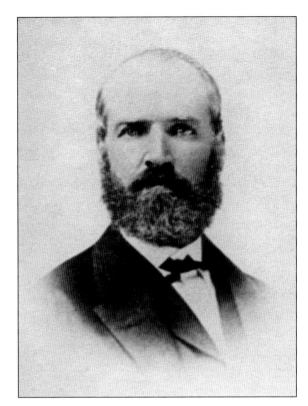

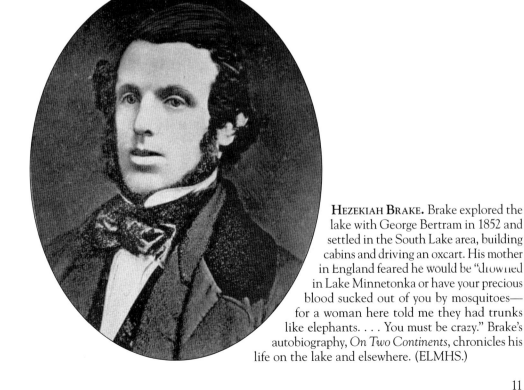

HEZEKIAH BRAKE. Brake explored the lake with George Bertram in 1852 and settled in the South Lake area, building cabins and driving an oxcart. His mother in England feared he would be "drowned in Lake Minnetonka or have your precious blood sucked out of you by mosquitoes—for a woman here told me they had trunks like elephants. . . . You must be crazy." Brake's autobiography, On Two Continents, chronicles his life on the lake and elsewhere. (ELMHS.)

11

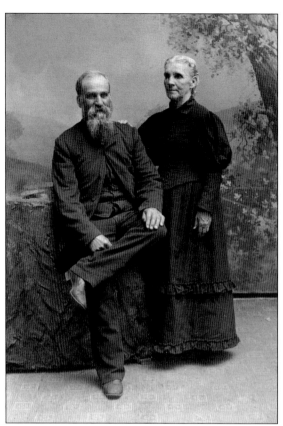

AMOS AND SUSAN CHOWEN GRAY. In 1853, millwright and carpenter Amos Gray settled in Minnetonka Township on what is now known as Grays Bay and built the first sawmill and store in Wayzata the following year. He was the overseer of highways and served on the town board. His home (below) still stands on Minnetonka Boulevard. (Left, DGS; below, MTHS.)

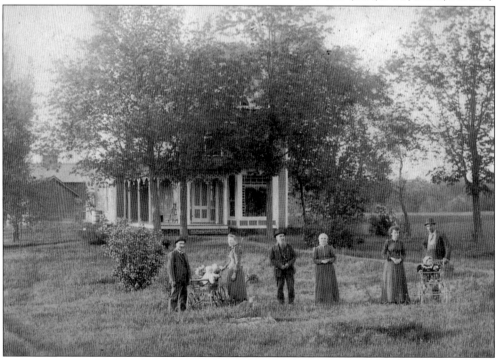

WILLIAM CHOWEN. Settling in Minnetonka Township in 1853, Chowen built his home in the Groveland area. He donated land for the first school in the township in 1854 and was elected to the first state legislature in 1857. Following Civil War service, Chowen returned to a life of civic duty in the lake area. He died in Minnetonka and is buried in Groveland Cemetery. (ELMHS.)

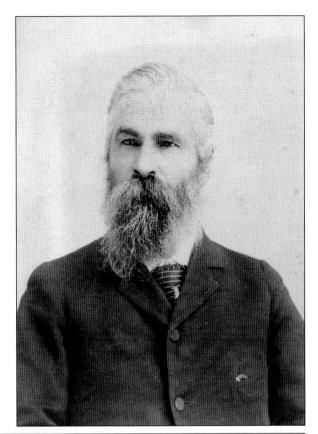

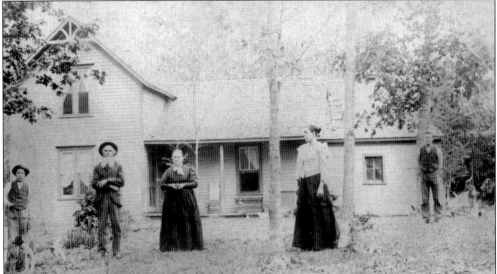

JOSEPH CHOWEN FAMILY, DEEPHAVEN. From left to right are Mac, Joseph, Caroline, Annie, and Lew Chowen at their home in what is still known as Chowen's Corner. Chowen came to the area in 1854, and in 1880 began a nursery, planting trees in Deephaven and Minnetonka. It is said that an Indian trail passed by the house, and Chowen offered lodging in return for fish or game. All except Lew lived on the corner for their entire lives. (ELMHS.)

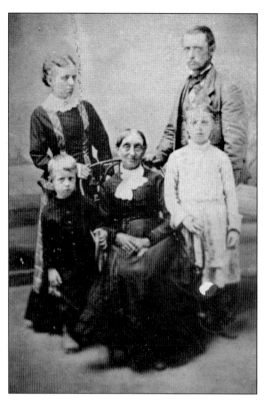

LYDIA FERGUSON HOLTZ WITH CHILDREN AND GRANDCHILDREN. New York school teachers Lydia and William Ferguson homesteaded in what is now Deephaven in 1854 with their two young children. In 1857, William fell through the ice and drowned, and Lydia endured a lifelong struggle to keep her home and family together. Her diaries detail her hardships and tell much about early Lake Minnetonka. Her family continued their Linwood ties for over 100 years. (ELMHS.)

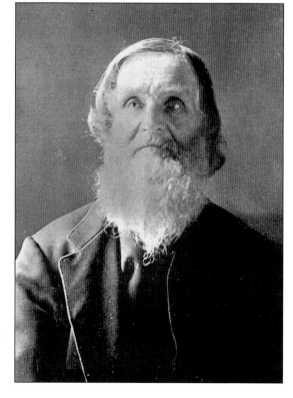

JOHN STEVENS HARRINGTON. Arriving in what is now Ferndale about 1854, Harrington, with his wife and daughter, purchased 160 acres for $2.50 per acre. He built Lake Side Home for his family and added 16 rooms, renaming it Harrington Inn, the first summer hotel in Wayzata. The area later became Harrington Farms. Harrington also laid out Wayzata's first road, calling it Harrington Road. (WZHS.)

WILLIAM B. MORSE. Morse homesteaded on Big Island and built the first house there in 1855. The island bore his name for a time, and he later operated a popular island campground. Morse ran afoul of the law in 1880 when he was convicted of selling liquor without a license. Five generations of his family are buried in Excelsior's Oak Hill Cemetery. (ELMHS.)

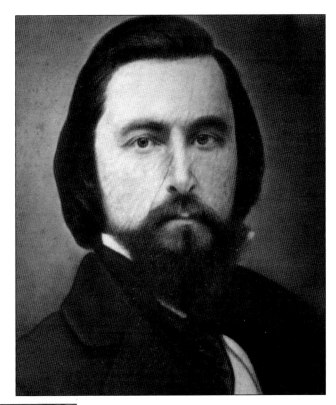

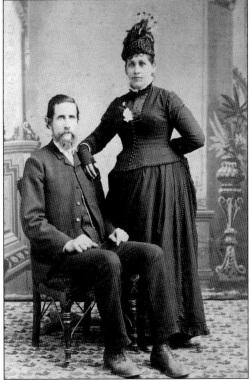

BENJAMIN AND MARY BRUNK KEESLING. Arriving in Wayzata in 1856, the Keeslings were among the town's first settlers. Following crop losses after the 1857 grasshopper invasion, Keesling and his brother-in-law worked digging ginseng. Payment in gold for this wonder plant offered financial recovery. Benjamin managed the Dudley Hotel, owned by William and Anna Dudley, and served as a town board member, justice of the peace, and school board director. (WZHS.)

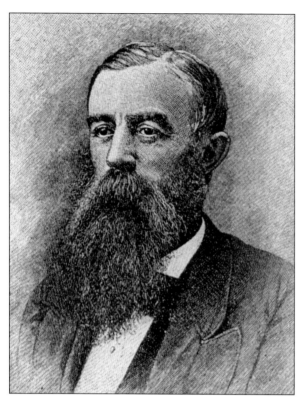

THE HALSTED BROTHERS. Capt. Frank Halsted (left) homesteaded in Minnetrista on Halsted Bay in 1855. After Civil War service, he built a cabin on the west Upper Lake known as the Hermitage. A learned and gentle man, Halsted served as Minnetrista's first justice of the peace, assisted with lake navigation improvements, and built the steamer *Mary* in 1876. After the *Mary* proved a financial disappointment, Halsted drowned himself and was buried near his home. Maj. George Halsted (below) arrived at the Hermitage to settle his brother's affairs and remained. Like his brother, he welcomed visitors to his home and continued to operate the *Mary*, whose boiler exploded in 1880, killing four people. The Hermitage was destroyed by fire with George inside in 1901, and he was buried beside his brother. The family name is sometimes spelled Halstead. (Both, ELMHS.)

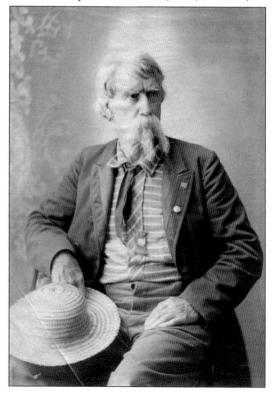

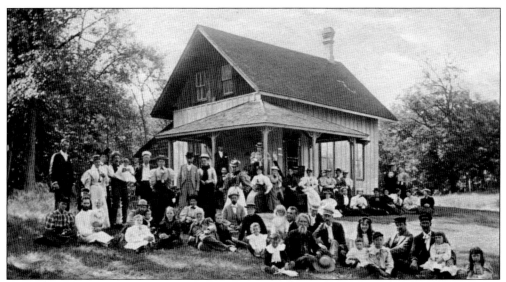

THE HERMITAGE, MINNETRISTA. Capt. Frank Halsted's cottage was built in 1866 on the lake overlooking Crane Island and was filled with exotic curiosities. It was a regular stop on lake tours and was visited by hundreds. After Halsted's death in 1876, his brother George, seated center front, lived there until 1901, when he died in the fire that destroyed the Hermitage. The property is now a residential subdivision, and the Halsteds' unmarked graves are believed to remain. (ELMHS.)

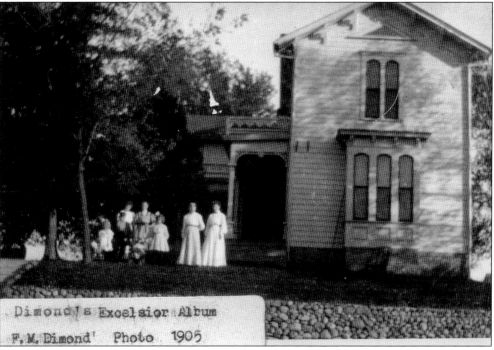

Dimond's Excelsior Album
F. M. Dimond Photo 1905

JAMES H. CLARK HOUSE, EXCELSIOR, 1905. In 1858, Clark came from prospecting in California to Excelsior and built this house. After Civil War service, he held several public offices in Excelsior and served in the state legislature in 1877. His home was enlarged and became the J.H. Clark Boarding House in the 1870s, with room for 30 guests. It stands at 371 Water Street as the Bird House Inn. (ELMHS.)

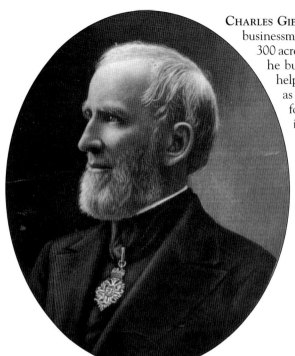

CHARLES GIBSON. In 1877, Gibson, an attorney and businessman from St. Louis, Missouri, purchased 300 acres from Carsons to Robinsons Bay, where he built Northome, his summer estate. He helped establish the Lake Minnetonka area as a national tourist destination by lobbying for road, railroad, and lake navigation improvements and actively promoting it to Southerners. (ELMHS.)

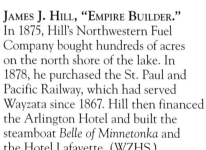

JAMES J. HILL, "EMPIRE BUILDER." In 1875, Hill's Northwestern Fuel Company bought hundreds of acres on the north shore of the lake. In 1878, he purchased the St. Paul and Pacific Railway, which had served Wayzata since 1867. Hill then financed the Arlington Hotel and built the steamboat *Belle of Minnetonka* and the Hotel Lafayette. (WZHS.)

GEORGE A. BRACKETT. The former mayor of Minneapolis and first commodore of the Lake Minnetonka Yacht Club, Brackett purchased Starvation Point on the lake's north shore in 1880. Now Bracketts Point, many of the early sailing regattas were held off this same point. Brackett's famous bean recipe, baked in cast-iron pots underground for 24 hours, served over 100 hungry sailors after races. (ELMHS.)

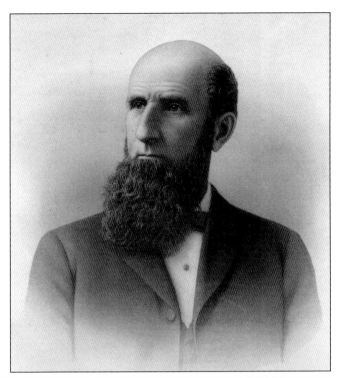

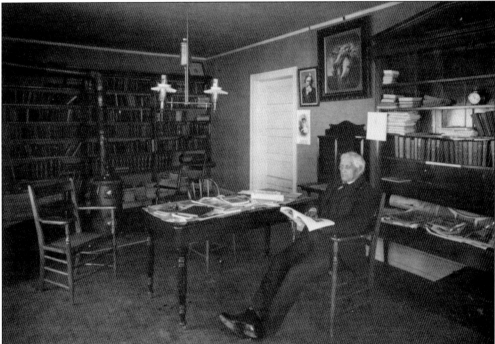

MILES DICKEY, WAYZATA LIBRARY. Dickey moved to Wayzata in 1880 and immersed himself in community life as a leader in the Temperance Society, founder of the town's first church in 1881, and founder of its public library in 1895. The library moved to the new village hall in 1905 (pictured) and remained there until the building burned in 1955. (WZHS.)

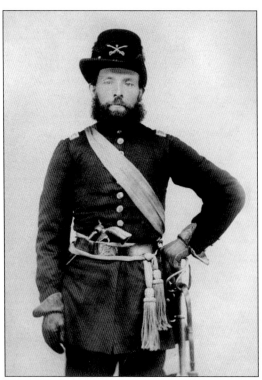

CAPT. ANTON P. KOEHLER, 1864. Koehler and his family came by train to Wayzata in 1880 and crossed the frozen lake by sleigh to their Halsted Bay homestead. Koehler is remembered for donating an acre of his farm for the area's first cemetery. His sons William and George were lifetime residents of Mound and active in its early progress. Koehler descendants continue to live in the area. (WTHS.)

MOORE CABIN, MOUND, C. 1911. Charles and Sophia Moore purchased their shoreline property on Cooks Bay from Frank and Adella Moore Carman in 1877. The Moores enlarged the cabin to accommodate visits from their 13 children and numerous grandchildren. Their son John built an additional structure in 1911 behind the house. The original cabin was moved 200 feet east and still exists within a remodeled home. (WTHS.)

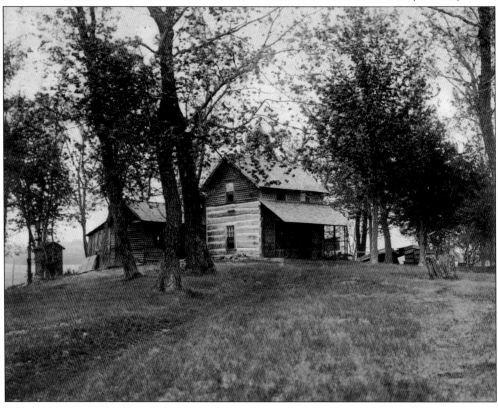

CAPT. ED WEST. Before arriving at Lake Minnetonka, West was a steamboat pilot on the Mississippi River. He came to Wayzata in 1881 and is remembered as the pilot of the *Belle of Minnetonka*. In 1889, he became owner of the Minnetonka House in Wayzata, renaming it the West Hotel. Upon his death in 1904, West was hailed as the oldest upper river pilot in active service. (WZHS.)

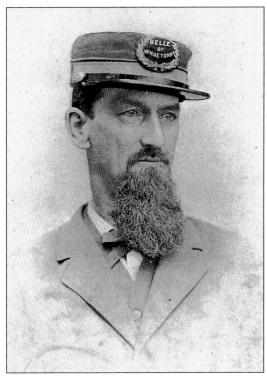

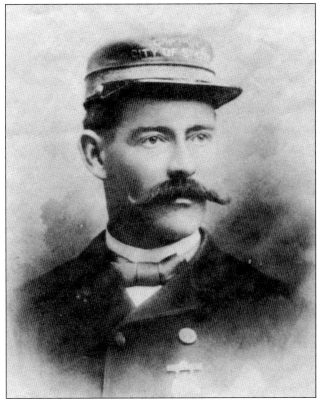

CAPT. JOHN R. JOHNSON. A Norwegian immigrant, Johnson was a captain of the two largest steamers on the lake during his long career—the *City of Saint Louis* and the *Belle of Minnetonka*, as well as many other boats. He was a popular and heroic figure, saving lives on the lake and showing many kindnesses to strangers. A memorial stands in his honor in Excelsior. (ELMHS.)

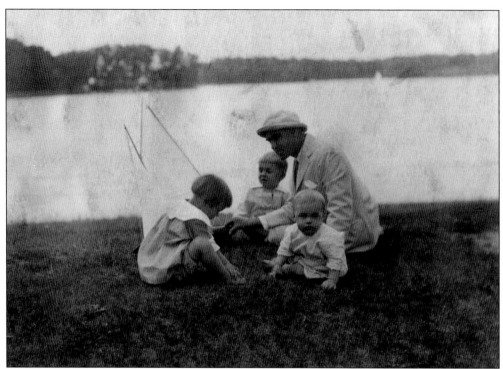

WARD BURTON AND CHILDREN, DEEPHAVEN. Burton began to spend childhood summers on Lake Minnetonka with his father, Hazen, and family in 1883. Celebrating outdoor activities with their neighbors was a family tradition, and Burton, "the Compleat Sportsman" excelled at them, too. He played tennis, raced yachts, cross-country skied, and played field and ice hockey. (ELMHS.)

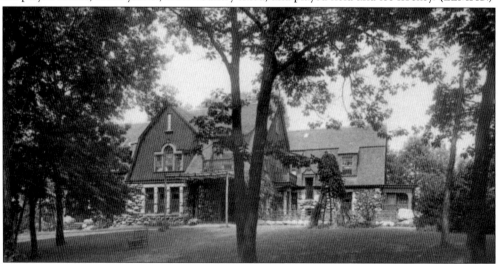

CHIMO, DEEPHAVEN. This massive house with seven fireplaces was designed by William Channing Whitney in 1892 for Hazen Burton, owner of the Plymouth Clothing Company in Minneapolis. Burton named his home Chimo, meaning "friendly" in some Canadian Indian languages. The 90-acre estate on Carsons Bay was near the railroad for easy city commuting. It had a chip-and-putt golf course, several grass tennis courts, and a large boathouse for the family sailboat fleet. The house still stands. (ELMHS.)

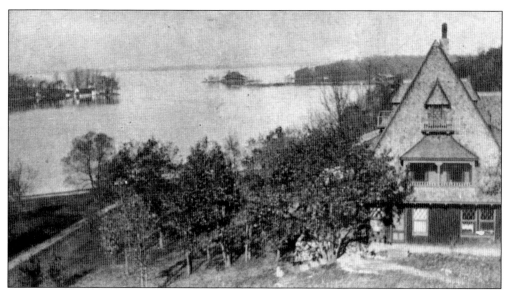

GLOOSKAP, DEEPHAVEN, 1894. A guest cottage on the Hazen Burton estate, Glooskap was named for an Indian legend trickster. Designed by William Channing Whitney, Glooskap has been extensively remodeled and is still standing. (ELMHS.)

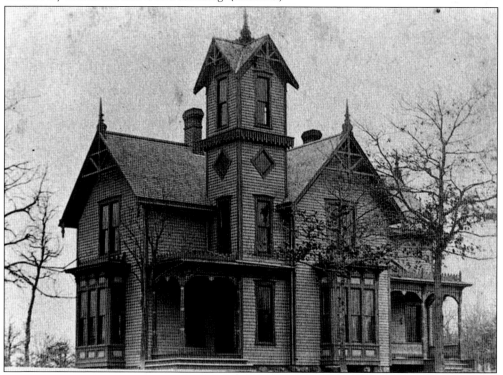

BURWELL HOUSE, MINNETONKA MILLS. Charles Burwell, manager of the Minnetonka Mills Company from 1874 to 1884, built his house along Minnehaha Creek in 1883. The property, purchased from the mill, had a large millpond with a dock and boathouse located in front of the house. The home still stands on McGinty Road and is listed in the National Register of Historic Places. Today it is operated as a museum by the Minnetonka Historical Society. (MTHS.)

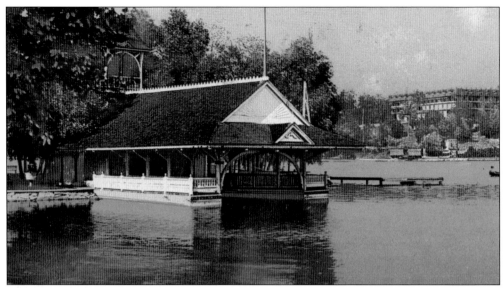

CRESTHAVEN BOATHOUSE, COTTAGEWOOD, C. 1891. In 1883, brothers Latimus and Lysander Moore of Kansas City, Kansas, hired Minneapolis architect Carl Struck to design the boathouse on their Grandview Point summer estate. The Moore estate was sold in 1892 and subdivided after 1906, and the boathouse no longer exists. The Hotel St. Louis can be seen on the right. (WTHS.)

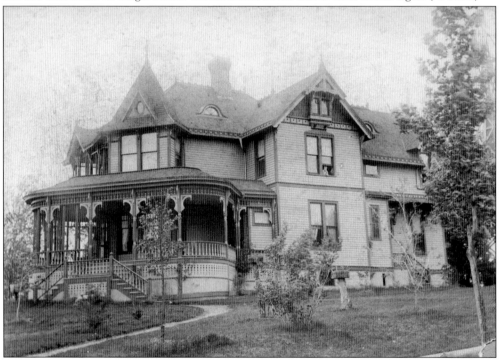

WYER LODGE, EXCELSIOR, 1894. James Wyer built his lodge in 1887 on three acres overlooking Excelsior Bay. It was the grandest house in town, with 12 rooms, six fireplaces, and two porches, plus an orchard, vineyard, and lawns sprawling to the lake. Standing on Mill Street, it has been used as apartments, offices, a bed and breakfast, and today, condominiums. It is listed in the National Register of Historic Places. (ELMHS.)

THE BLEGEN HOUSE, ORONO. In 1887, Prof. John Blegen built his summer home along the west arm of Lake Minnetonka. The property included a summer kitchen, a shower house, a windmill that pumped lake water, and an orchard. Blegen and his neighbors, members of the Saga Hill Colony, were professors, ministers, bankers, and professional men with ties to Augsburg Seminary and College. (WTHS.)

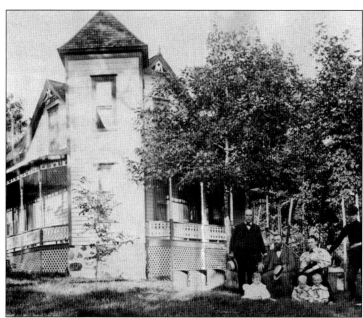

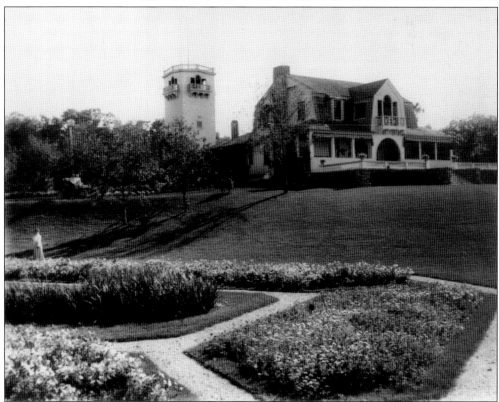

OLD ORCHARD, TONKA BAY, 1905. John F. Wilcox hired architect George Bertrand to design his summer home in 1897. Built on the old Minnesota State Fruit Farm, the 86-acre estate was known for its formal flower gardens, Ayrshire cattle, and chickens. It was later run as an inn, and Wilcox's widow sold it after his death. It is no longer standing. (HCL.)

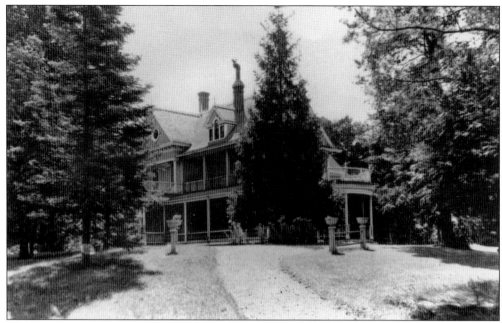

OLAF SEARLE HOME, BIG ISLAND. In 1891, Searle built the first large estate on the island. The house had 21 rooms, several chimneys, steam heat, and gas lights. It was yellow with white trim and had a large front porch, plus orchards and a Japanese garden. Searle had a channel dug, cutting Big Island in two sections, and it remains a boat passage today. The house burned in 1932. (ELMHS.)

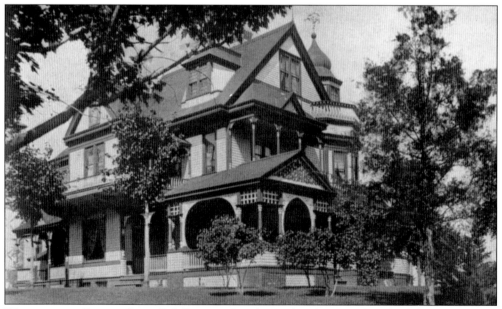

WILLKOMMEN, ORONO. Grain Belt Brewery founder Frederick Noerenberg built his estate on 73 acres overlooking Crystal and Maxwell Bays in 1890. In 1972, his last surviving child died with a will stating that the home be razed and the property maintained as a public garden by the Hennepin County Park System. Today, the formal gardens and gazebo boathouse are a popular wedding location. (ELMHS.)

NORTHRUP ESTATE, WAYZATA.
This home was designed by
William Channing Whitney in
1894 for William Northrup in
Ferndale. The Greek Revival
architecture showcased a Doric-
columned entrance, elaborate
European-style gardens, and
an expansive lawn reaching
the lake. Northrup named
his estate Bonsyde, and locals
nicknamed it "the White
House of Minnesota." It was
demolished in 2013. (WZHS.)

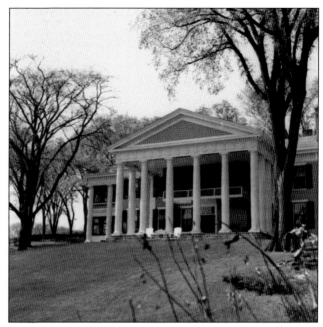

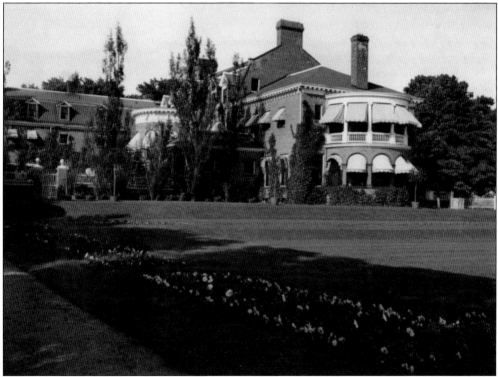

HIGHCROFT, WAYZATA. Built in 1895, Highcroft was designed by William Channing Whitney
for Frank Peavey. The manor and 111-acre estate in Ferndale had 30 rooms, spacious lawns, and
gardens, and was a working dairy farm. The home's jewel was the 40-by-60-foot great hall with
fireplaces and a grand stairway. In 1953, the home was demolished and the land was sold and
subdivided. (WZHS.)

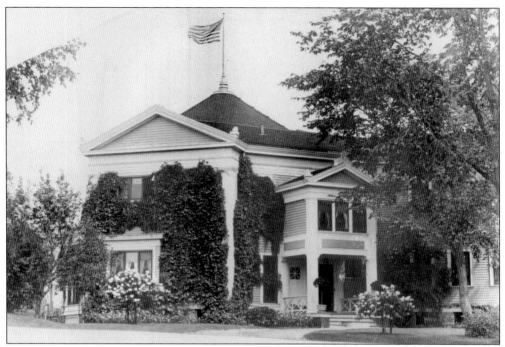

KATAHDIN, DEEPHAVEN. At the entrance to Carsons Bay, atop a hill on Swifts Point, stood the Lucian Swift home, built for year-round residency in 1898. Designed in the Classical Revival style, Katahdin was named for the highest mountain in Maine. It had a 30-foot central hall with a billiard table in the middle that doubled as a banquet table. Swift was manager and co-owner of the *Minneapolis Journal*. (HCL.)

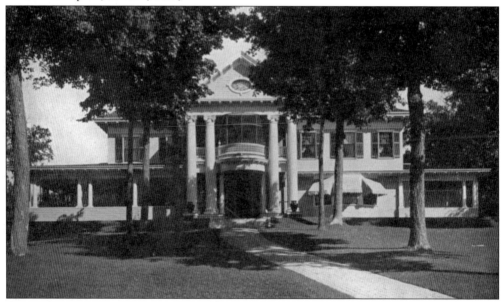

CEDARHURST, DEEPHAVEN. In 1901, Russell M. Bennett hired architect William Channing Whitney to design his house on property that had been part of Charles Gibson's Northome estate. Built to take advantage of the best lake views, Cedarhurst had seven bedrooms, two baths, a large stable, and a bathhouse. (ELMHS.)

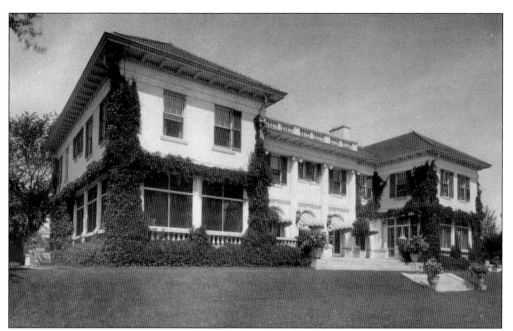

BELFORD, WAYZATA. Located on the highest point in Ferndale, Belford was designed by William Channing Whitney in 1907 as a summer home for James Stroud Bell. It was named for Bell and his wife, Sallie Ford, and is of Neoclassical design, with wings on either side of a center entrance. Its white stucco exterior against a red tile roof prompted boaters viewing it from Wayzata Bay to give it the nickname "Red Top." The grounds were extensively landscaped, with a swimming pool and several gardens, including a Japanese water garden with goldfish. In 1912, *The House Beautiful* magazine commented, "such estates as Belford prove more and more the foresight of American men of wealth and taste." The house is still standing. (Both, WZHS.)

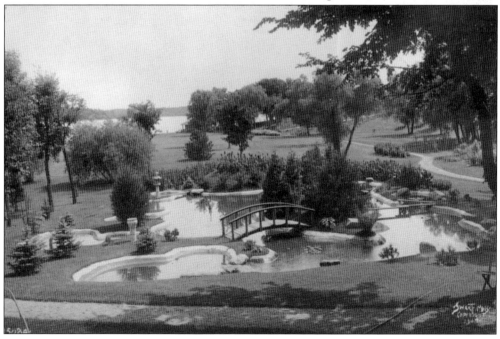

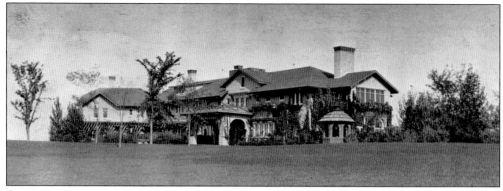

GOODRICH ESTATE, ZUMBRA HEIGHTS. Minneapolis Street Railway Company executive Calvin Goodrich hired Leroy Buffington in 1909 to design his summer residence on the previous site of the Palmer House. Overlooking Smithtown Bay, the 17-acre estate was sold in 1919 to C.F. Hoffman for $100,000. The home is no longer standing. (ELMHS.)

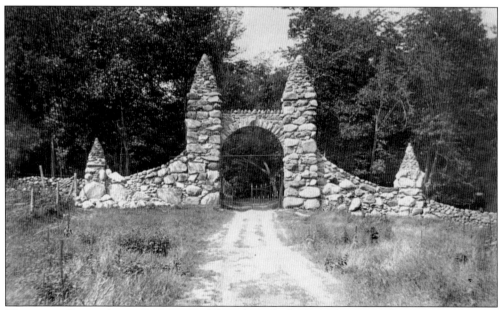

NORTHOME STONE ARCH, DEEPHAVEN. Thought to be built in the 1870s, this arch stood as the gateway to Charles Gibson's estate, Northome. The left side of the structure was partially removed to accommodate traffic, but it otherwise remains standing and largely unchanged on Northome Road. (ELMHS.)

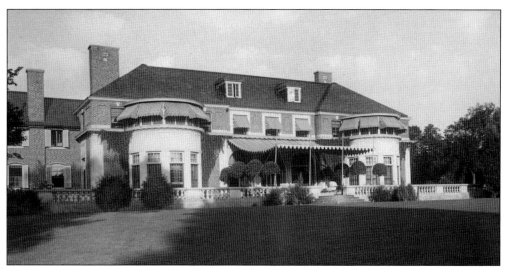

WALDEN, DEEPHAVEN. Walter Douglas and his wife, Mahala, hired Chicago architect Howard Van Doren Shaw to design their French Renaissance mansion in 1909. On the voyage home following a European shopping vacation, Walter drowned when the *Titanic* sank in 1912. Mahala returned to live in Walden until her death in 1945. The estate was subdivided in the 1950s, and the house remains a private residence. (WC.)

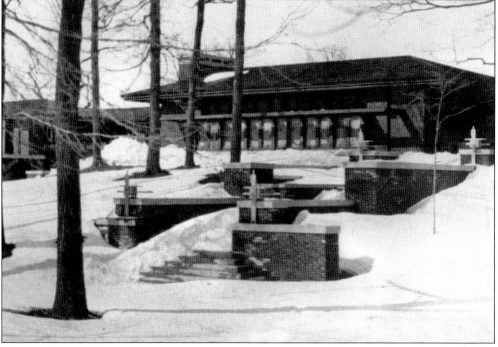

FRANCIS LITTLE HOUSE, DEEPHAVEN. Designed by Frank Lloyd Wright and completed in 1914 as a summer residence, this was considered one of Wright's last great Prairie School designs. The house was winterized by Little's daughter, who, frustrated by the ownership challenges of a Wright house, sold it to the Metropolitan Museum of Art, where its living room is on permanent exhibit. Other parts of the house may be seen at the Minneapolis Institute of Arts and other museums. The remainder was demolished in 1972. (ELMHS.)

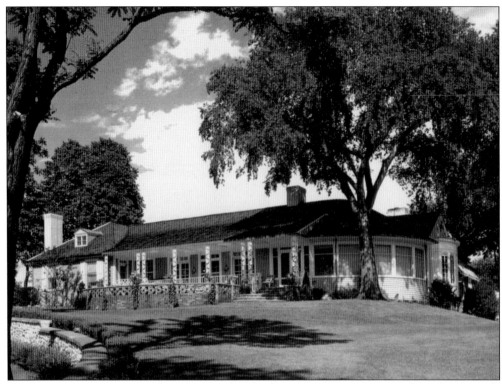

LOCUST HILLS, WAYZATA. Purchased in 1939 by Charles Baxter Sweatt, vice president of Honeywell, Locust Hills was developed into a country estate with lavish gardens, a tennis court, a riding ring, pastures for thoroughbred horses, and swans in the lagoon. The annual St. Martin's-by-the-Lake Country Fair was held on the grounds. In 2009, the property was developed into the Locust Hills residential community, and the house was razed. (WZHS.)

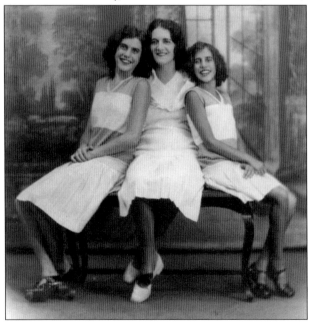

THE ANDREWS SISTERS, 1930S. From left to right, singers Maxene, LaVerne, and Patty Andrews summered in Mound with relatives from 1917 through the 1960s. Their careers began with a 1931 audition at the Orpheum Theater in Minneapolis. They later performed with Bing Crosby, Bob Hope, Glenn Miller, and Guy Lombardo. Remembered for their World War II USO tours, they sold over 75 million records, starred in 16 movies, and were one of the most popular groups of the 20th century. (ELMHS.)

Two

SPIRES AND TOWERS

Faithful gatherings around Lake Minnetonka were an integral part of village building, and the settlers also looked forward to resting on Sunday and socializing. Excelsior's Congregational church, led by Rev. Charles Galpin in 1853, held services in a hotel parlor, a schoolhouse, and the second floor of a store until a church was built in 1871. The Episcopalians met near St. Albans Bay in a log church in 1855. In the early days, Wayzata residents were visited by circuit preachers, later attending church in Parkers Lake, and finally building the Congregational Church of Christ in Wayzata in 1881. In the Upper Lake area, the first established church was founded by the Methodists in 1890, followed by the Catholics in 1909. Other denominations met regularly in homes of the faithful, ministered to by circuit preachers, until they could build their own permanent structures.

Lake Minnetonka villagers and farmers considered education a priority, conducting classes in private homes until schoolhouses were built. Excelsior's first schoolhouse opened in 1854, and the town became an independent school district in 1899. Wayzata's first log school building was built in 1858, the same year School District 52 was organized. In 1880, the town built its first brick school. In Minnetonka, school was held in a log building used until 1871, when it was replaced by a frame building. Following Minnesota statehood in 1858, territories were divided into townships, with land allocated for schools. In 1860, Hennepin County commissioners accepted Frank Halsted's petition to form School District 85 in Minnetrista, with John Carman of Cooks Bay as the first superintendent. Rural school buildings dotted the area, including Stubbs Bay, Orono, Spring Park, and Tonka Bay.

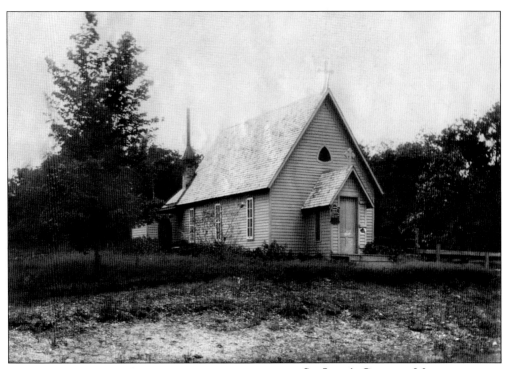

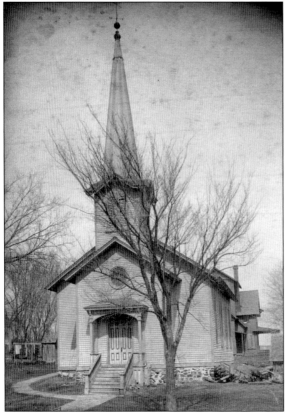

St. John's Church, Minnetonka. Consecrated in 1858, St. John's stood near Minnetonka Boulevard and Baker Road. Originally Episcopalian, it was later served by circuit preachers of various faiths and used for secular and educational purposes. It was reclaimed by Episcopalians in 1871; one year later, two services were held two Sundays monthly with catechism afterwards, for 25 families. By 1918, it was vacant and burned to the ground. (ELMHS.)

The First Congregational Church of Excelsior. Excelsior pioneer Rev. Charles Galpin organized the First Independent Church of Excelsior and Chanhassen in July 1853. Until the building was completed in 1871 for $4,500, members met in homes, a hotel, a store, and a school. It was demolished in 1970 and replaced at the same location with the Congregational Church of Excelsior. (ELMHS.)

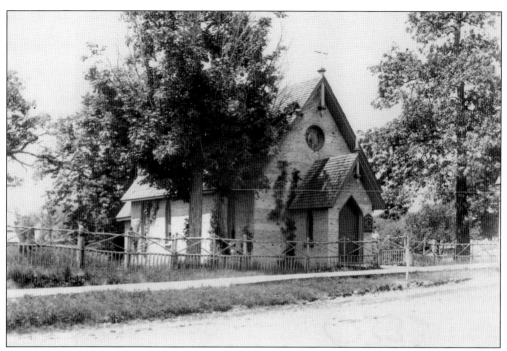

TRINITY EPISCOPAL CHURCH, EXCELSIOR. Completed in 1863 for $1,000 with Lake Minnetonka stones and Shakopee lime, Trinity Mission Episcopal Chapel was called "a model of beauty and cheapness" by Minnesota's first Episcopal bishop, Henry B. Whipple. It is the oldest church building in Excelsior and the oldest Episcopal church in continuous use in Minnesota. Originally constructed on Third Street (above), it was moved in 1907 (below) to its present location on Second Street to make room for the streetcar tracks. (Above, HCL; below, ELMHS.)

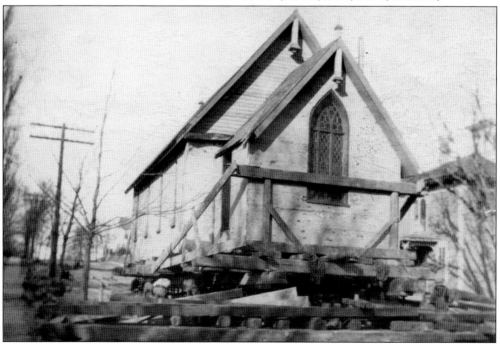

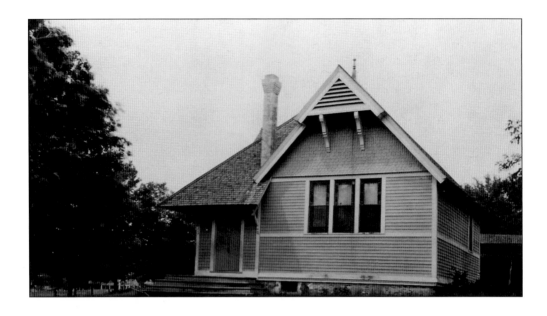

WAYZATA CONGREGATIONAL CHURCH. Wayzata's first church (above) was built in 1881 at the corner of Rice Street and Walker Avenue. The gray clapboard building with white trim was approximately 30 feet square, and its interior had barely enough space for a pump organ, pulpit, and two stoves for heat. It began with 12 charter members and was officially called the Congregational Church of Christ in Wayzata. In 1882, the members purchased a bell from Clinton Meneely Bell Company for $80. In 1911, a new church was designed by Harry Wild Jones, incorporating the older wooden building into the new structure. In 1916, the church burned due to defective electrical wiring, and a new one was built (below) using the old design. It stands today as the Unitarian Universalist Church of Minnetonka. (Both, WZHS.)

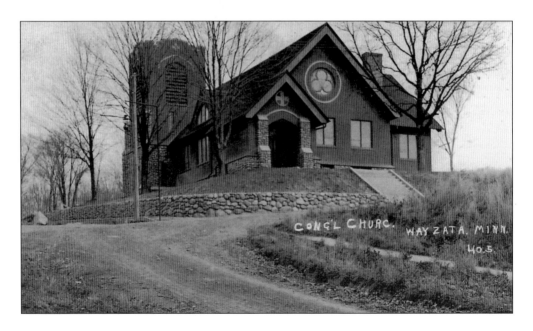

METHODIST EPISCOPAL CHURCH, EXCELSIOR. This church was built on George Street in 1885. After many improvements and expansions, the congregation built a larger church, Excelsior United Methodist Church, on Highway 7 in 1958, and the old church was demolished. (ELMHS.)

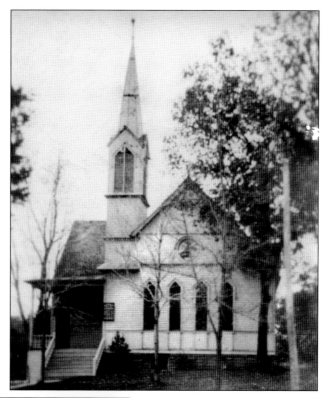

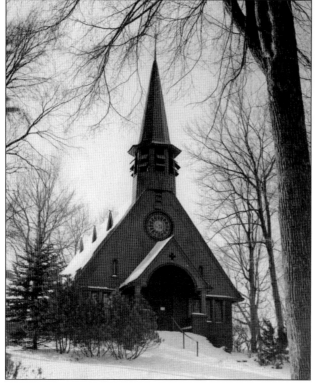

CAMP MEMORIAL CHAPEL, MINNETONKA BEACH. George and Lucy Camp financed this chapel in 1888, designed by Cass Gilbert and facing Lafayette Bay. It was dedicated to Camp's three infant daughters who died, and the first service held was the wedding of their surviving daughter. The family then donated the church to the Minnesota Diocese of the Episcopal Church. In 1950, it was moved to its present location and renamed St. Martin's-by-the-Lake Episcopal Church. (SML.)

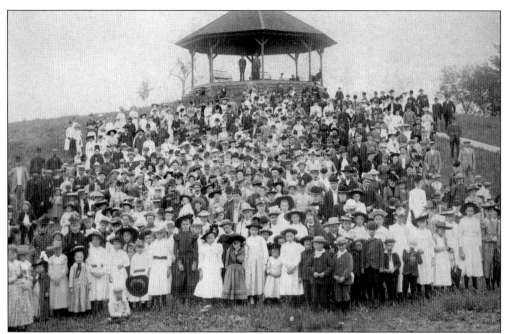

SUNDAY SCHOOL PICNIC, SPRING PARK, 1890. A summer Sunday School class from the Minneapolis Swedish Mission Tabernacle congregation ventured to Lake Minnetonka for a Saturday picnic. The congregation was shepherded by revivalist Erik Skogsbergh. (HHM.)

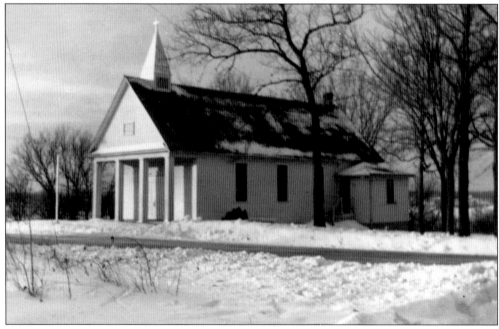

SWEDISH FRIENDS MISSION, ORONO. In 1901, charismatic minister Erik Skogsbergh preached a doctrine of practical Christianity and founded Fairview Park Tabernacle to serve the area's growing Swedish population. He attracted followers traveling by train and steamboat for weekend gatherings he called Bible Expositions. The congregation continues to worship as Fairview Covenant Church near Jennings Bay. (HHM.)

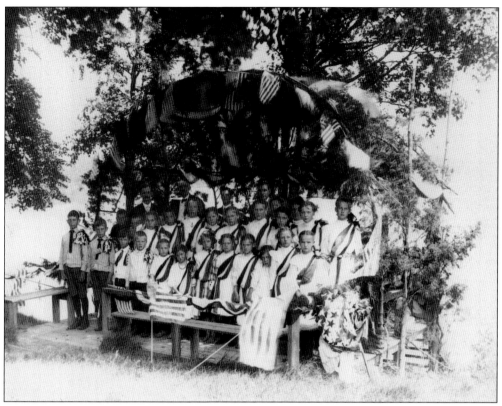

MOUND ASSEMBLY GROUNDS. The assembly campus on the Highlands of west Cooks Bay was a popular gathering site for the Baptist Church Annual Summer Assembly from 1900 through the 1950s. Revivals featured Billy Sunday and Billy Graham, and extra trains were scheduled to accommodate the hundreds of attendees. Tent spaces, a dining hall, hotel, auditorium, and cottages for lease filled the grounds. Morning devotions and religious education, like the 1910 photograph above of Judge Fish with a Sunday School class, led to afternoons of outdoor water fun. Days ended with a strict lights-out at 10:00 p.m. Today, the property is a residential subdivision with original campus cottages still standing. (Above, HCL; below, WTHS.)

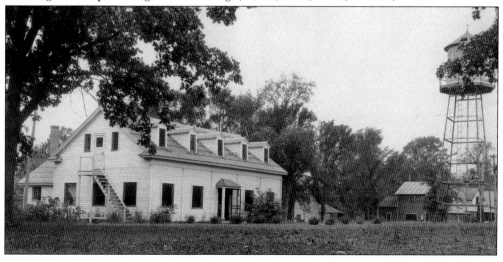

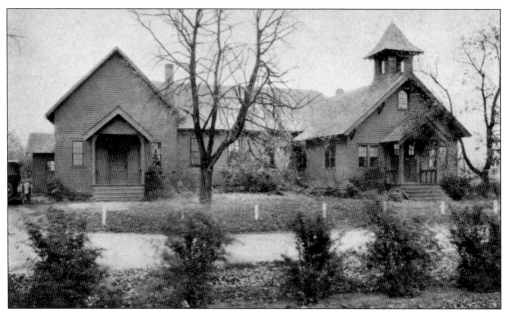

MINNEWASHTA CHURCH, SHOREWOOD. Minnewashta Union Congregational Church was built in an orchard in 1916. It was moved to Smithtown Road in 1921 and attached to the right side of the vacated schoolhouse built there in 1896. This building was razed in 1993, and the congregation built a new church on the same site. (ELMHS.)

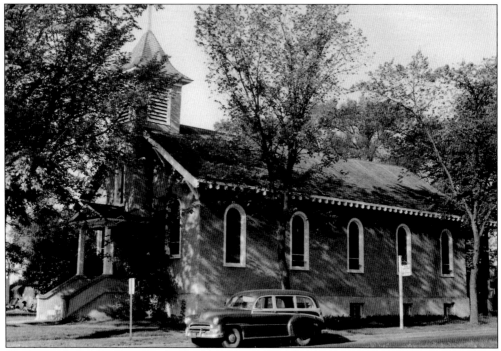

ST. BARTHOLOMEW'S CATHOLIC CHURCH OF WAYZATA. The parish of St. Bartholomew's was built in 1916, and the first mass was celebrated on Christmas Day. The church was grey stucco with white trim and named after its founding pastor, Rev. George Bartholomew Scheffold. St. Bart's, as the locals call it, was lost to fire in 1964 and rebuilt. (WZHS.)

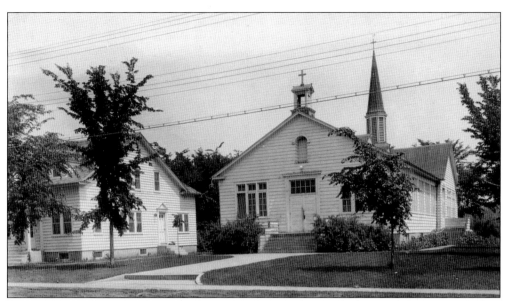

OUR LADY OF THE LAKE CATHOLIC CHURCH, MOUND. The parish's history began in 1909 when Bishop John Ireland instructed Fr. Francis Jager of Saint Bonifacius to build a permanent home for the area's Catholic population. In 1923, the parish built its second church, along Commerce Boulevard across from Langdon Lake. The building was razed in 1968, following the completion of a new church and school complex. (WTHS.)

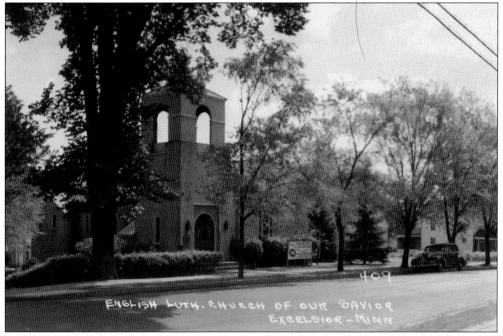

THE ENGLISH EVANGELICAL CHURCH OF OUR SAVIOR, EXCELSIOR, 1949. In 1924, nine church members met in Excelsior Town Hall and Trinity Episcopal Church until their basement chapel was completed on Second Street in 1927. The church building (pictured) was completed in 1933. In 1958, the congregation built and moved into a new building on Highway 7. The original church building was remodeled into apartments in the 1950s and still stands. (ELMHS.)

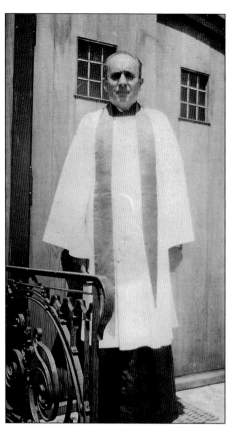

REV. MARTIN PAPE, REDEEMER LUTHERAN CHURCH, WAYZATA. In 1925, the first Lutheran service in Wayzata was held in its train depot. Pape had been making rounds each Sunday, preaching at Excelsior and Mound, adding Redeemer to his circuit in 1937. In 1938, the Wayzata congregation of 400 built their first church at the corner of Broadway Avenue and Rice Street. In 1954, they built a new church on Wayzata Boulevard, where it stands today. (WZHS.)

BETHEL METHODIST EPISCOPAL CHURCH. The first Mound congregation to build a church was Bethel in 1892. Property on Commerce Boulevard was donated by Lakeside Park Association, the Jennings family donated trees for lumber, and members worked on construction. Differing faiths held services at Bethel until their churches were built. In 1951, this church was dismantled and reassembled as a barn, and the congregation built a new church. (WTHS.)

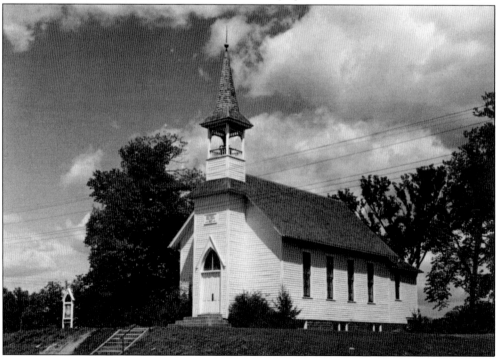

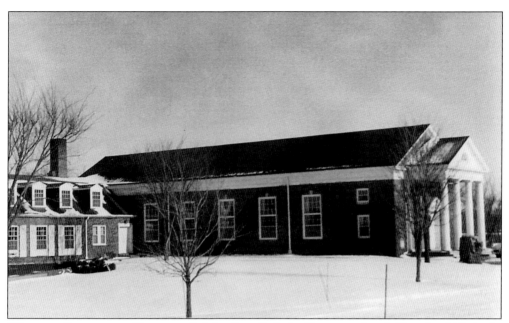

WAYZATA COMMUNITY CHURCH. Originally called the Congregational Church of Christ in Wayzata, the congregation voted unanimously in 1945 to build a new church on Wayzata Boulevard and Ferndale Avenue, changing its name to Wayzata Community Church. It was dedicated on November 27, 1949, and served 600 members. After several additions, including a steeple that can be seen for miles, it is home to 3,000 members today. (WZHS.)

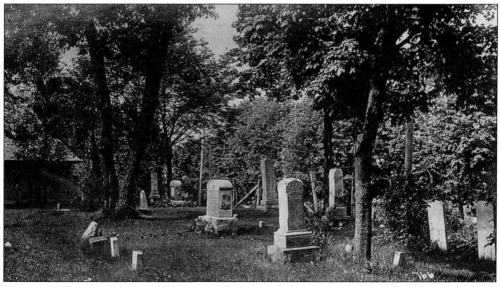

WAYZATA'S OLDEST CEMETERY. The town's first cemetery is north of its first church on the corner of Wayzata Boulevard and Walker Avenue. Originally known as Burying Hill, the official plat was recorded on November 1882. The first person to be buried in this cemetery was Hannah Garrison, mother of Oscar Garrison, one of Wayzata's founders. The cemetery remains an important landmark linking the town to its past. (WZHS.)

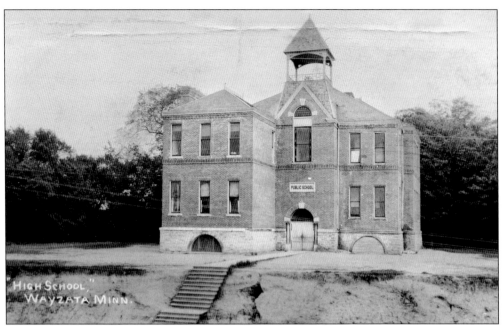

WAYZATA'S FIRST BRICK SCHOOL. Built in 1880, the red brick school atop Schoolhouse Hill facing Rice Street (above) held classes for the younger students on the first floor (below), and was also used as a community gathering space. The second level for upper grades had a dividing wall allowing for room size changes. By 1890, grades one through eight had 105 students, and a two-year high school curriculum was added in 1898. The school was demolished in 1910, and a larger school was built at the same location. (Both, WZHS.)

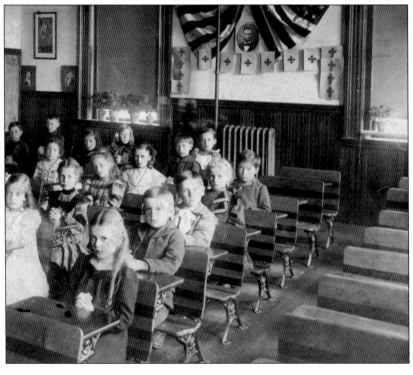

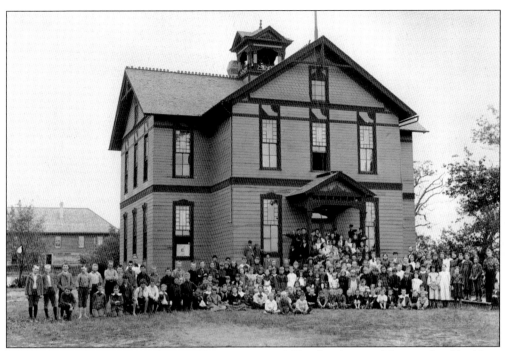

EXCELSIOR'S FOURTH PUBLIC SCHOOL BUILDING, 1896. Excelsior's second frame school building (above) was built in 1882 for over $6,000 on what is now School Avenue, and by the 1883 winter term, enrollment reached 161 students. On the morning of February 8, 1899, the temperature dipped to 25 degrees below zero, and a fire started in the basement as the students gathered upstairs, warming themselves next to the heating registers. Alice Page, the superintendent's assistant, grabbed her camera, climbed on the roof of the church's horse shed across the street, and photographed the fire (below). The building was a total loss, but no injuries were reported. (Both, ELMHS.)

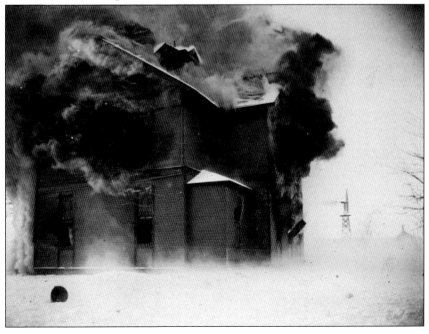

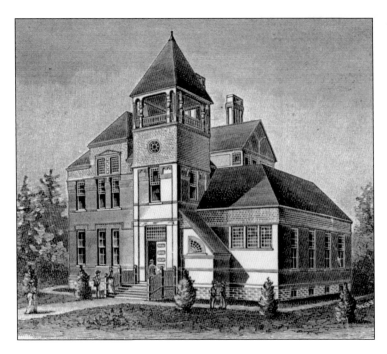

EXCELSIOR ACADEMY, GALPIN HALL. The cornerstone for this brick veneer building was laid in 1885. It was a private Christian school offering four years of college preparatory classes and stood between present-day Academy Avenue, Water Street, and Highway 7. By 1891, it was sold to Northwestern Christian College and offered four years of kindergarten beginning at age three, four years of college preparatory academics, and four years of college. The building burned in 1896. (ELMHS.)

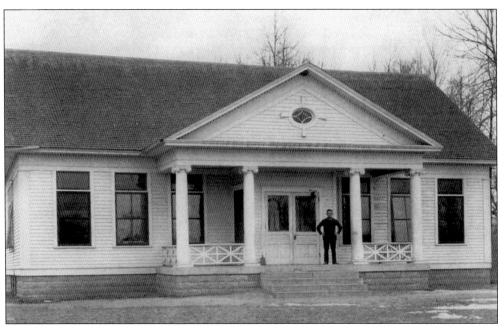

SPRING PARK SCHOOL. Serving grades one through four, this school was built in 1906. It had two rooms, two teachers, and outdoor toilets in the early years. Following the school's closure in 1963, the building was purchased for $1 by the Spring Park Community Improvement Association and donated to the community. It was moved and today stands as the Spring Park Village Hall. (WTHS.)

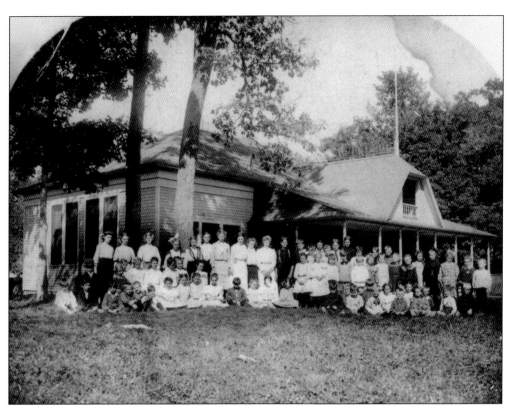

DEEPHAVEN PUBLIC SCHOOL. Built on land donated by the Burton family in 1892, this school on Vine Hill Road (above) expanded with the population, eventually adding a second level in 1916 (right) and including four years of high school. The building also served as a community center, housing church services, cultural events, and civic meetings. It was demolished in 1937. (Both, ELMHS.)

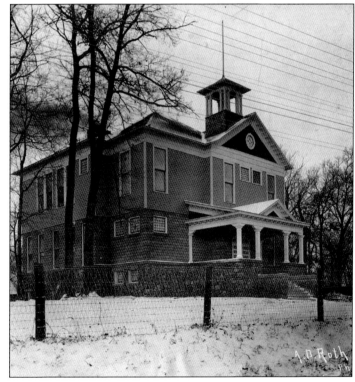

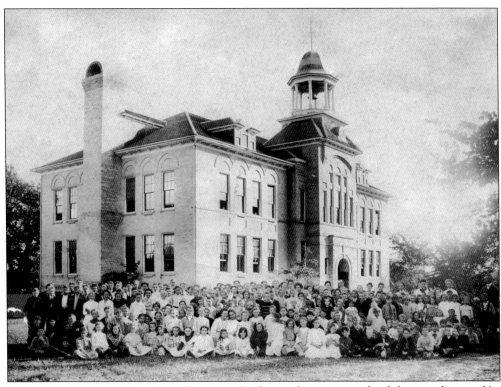

EXCELSIOR'S FIFTH PUBLIC SCHOOL BUILDING. Replacing the previous school that was destroyed by fire in 1899, this building (above) was completed the same year on the same site. By 1908, student enrollment numbered 345 in 12 grades. In 1915, it began serving the lower grades (below) when a new high school was built on Oak Street. From 1964 through 1995, it housed the Minnetonka School District administration offices. Today, it is used for private offices and is listed in the National Register of Historic Places. (Both, ELMHS.)

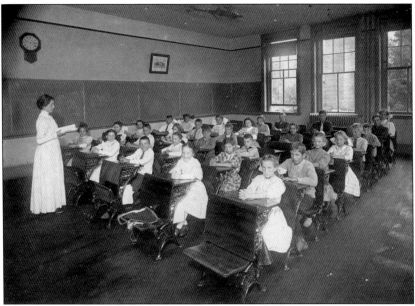

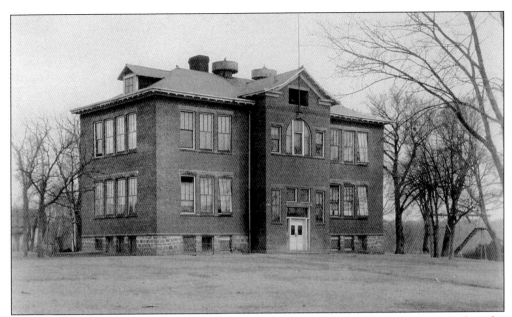

MOUND GRADE SCHOOL. The Little Red Schoolhouse was built in 1908 to accommodate the town's growing population. After 1917, kindergarten classes were added, and in 1942, it was retired from the education system and used as an ammunition box factory during World War II. In 1946, it was the first home of Mound Metalcraft, later known as Tonka Toys. Rendered unusable after fire damage, the building was demolished in 1964. (WTHS.)

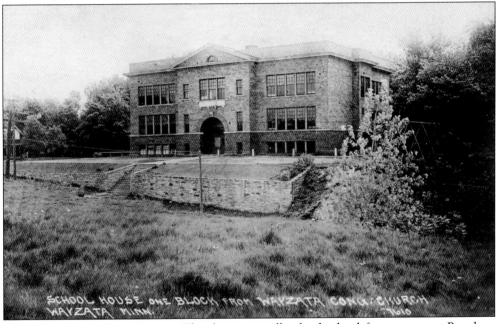

WAYZATA'S SECOND BRICK SCHOOL. This three-story yellow brick school, facing west onto Broadway Avenue, opened in 1910. The gymnasium in the basement was not big enough for a basketball game, but had enough space to practice shooting baskets. On February 10, 1920, it was destroyed by fire, and classes were held in the village hall and the Congregational church while a new school was being built. (WZHS.)

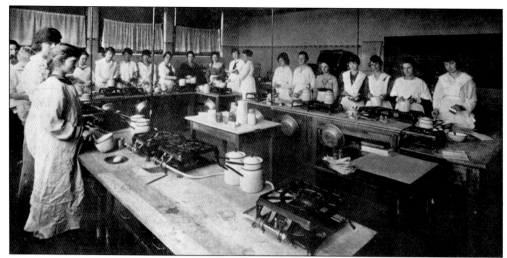

Wayzata's Domestic Science Class, 1915. Wayzata's school curriculum was considered modern and innovative. In addition to the art and science of cooking, students studied botany, geology, ancient and modern history, chemistry, physics, agriculture, commercial arithmetic, Latin, bookkeeping, and grammar. (WZHS.)

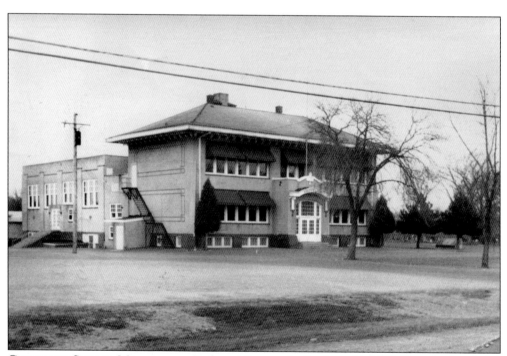

Groveland School, Minnetonka. Built on Minnetonka Boulevard in 1915, Groveland included two classrooms on the first floor and a large room used as a gymnasium, lunchroom, and community meeting space on the second level. The basement contained lockers, bathrooms, showers, and an industrial arts classroom. A new elementary school was built west of this building in 1958, and the old school was razed in 1976. (ELMHS.)

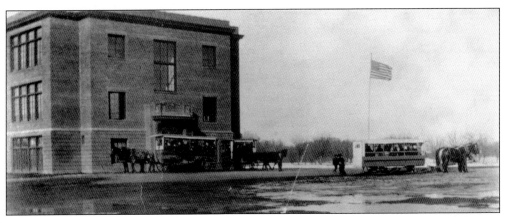

MINNEWASHTA SCHOOL, SHOREWOOD. Built on Smithtown Road in 1917, Minnewashta housed kindergarten through eighth grade in four rooms. Over the years, it was remodeled and the building was eventually incorporated into the new Minnewashta Elementary School. In the 1970s, it was demolished in preparation for a new building. (ELMHS.)

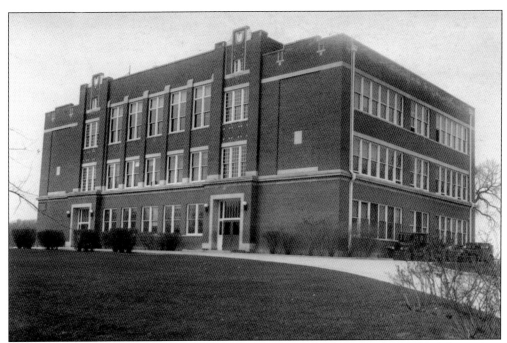

MOUND CONSOLIDATED HIGH SCHOOL. In 1917, District 85 built its first high school, located on Lynwood Boulevard, for students graduating from two dozen grade schools in the area. It had three levels with all the modern conveniences, including a 1,500-seat auditorium. Annexes were added in 1926 and 1938. By 2002, the 1938 building was in poor repair and sold, becoming a site for downtown redevelopment. (WTHS.)

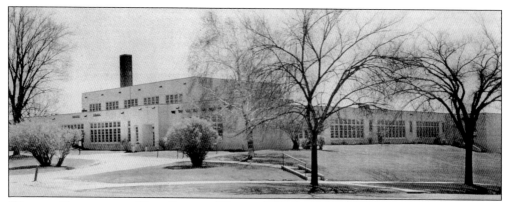

WAYZATA CONSOLIDATED HIGH SCHOOL (WIDSTEN). Dedicated in 1921, this pueblo-style building replaced the previous school that had burned on the same spot. For 30 years, this was Wayzata's only public school building. Following the death of high school principal Halvor Widsten, it was renamed Widsten Elementary School in 1953. In 1989, the Wayzata School Board sold the property to developers who razed the building in 1992. (WZHS.)

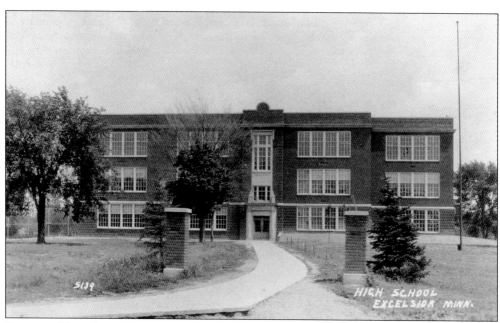

EXCELSIOR HIGH SCHOOL. In 1915, a three-story high school was built on Oak Street, and it burned in 1928 while many townspeople and volunteer firefighters were in Hopkins, Minnesota, cheering on the Excelsior High School basketball team. In 1929, the building pictured here was completed at the same location. It has served as a high school, junior high, and community center, and is now part of Excelsior Elementary School. (ELMHS.)

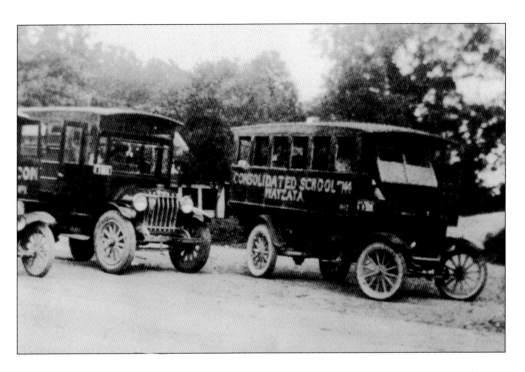

SCHOOL TRANSPORTATION. In the early days, Lake Minnetonka families depended on horse-drawn carriages, farm wagons, and their own feet for school transportation. Wayzata's motorized buses (above) used glass windows instead of the canvas curtains favored by rural schools. In 1921, Phelps Island resident John Iverson, who had cleared the island's first roads 20 years earlier, organized student transportation using his motorized wagon (below) for children whose families lived permanently on the island. Inside the bus, students sat on benches around the perimeter, facing the center, and entered and exited through a rear door to avoid startling horses, which were still common on the streets. (Above, WZHS; below, WTHS.)

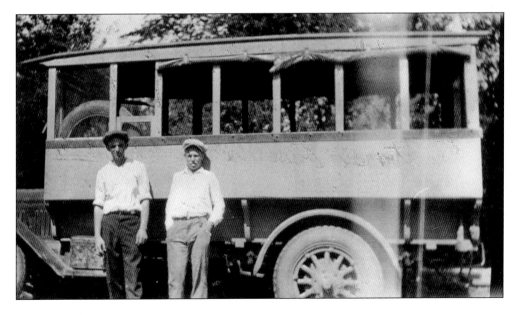

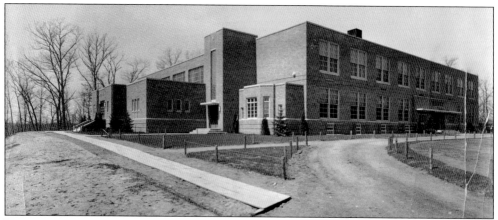

DEEPHAVEN PUBLIC SCHOOL, 1938. This building was built on the site of the previous school on Vine Hill Road. It has served as a high school, junior high, intermediate school, and elementary school. In the 1980s, it was Chapel Hill Academy, and today it is home to Minnetonka Community Education. (ELMHS.)

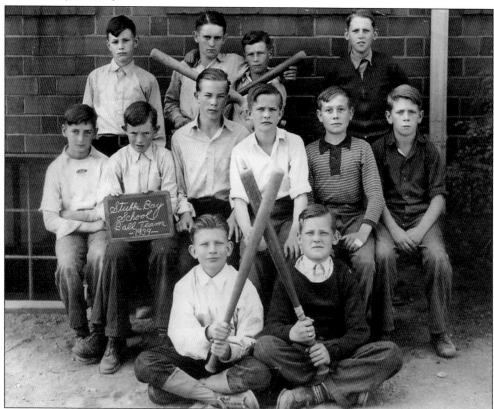

STUBBS BAY BALL TEAM, ORONO, 1939. The Stubbs Bay brick schoolhouse was a thriving learning center for nearly 50 years, built in 1912 across the street from the original 1893 wood-frame school. Ball team members pictured here are, from left to right, (first row) Junior Cirspinski and Charles Howe; (second row) Norman Bloom, Gerry Ross, Monte Nehrbass, Don Gronberg, Kerney Thies, and Richard Swanson; (third row) Charles Powell, David Bronson, John Dunn, and Everett White. Today the building is a private residence. (WTHS.)

Three

BY WATER, WHEEL, AND RAIL

Movement around and over Lake Minnetonka is a dynamic story of necessity, rivalry, and recreation. In 1855, Lucius Walker and Oscar Garrison started stagecoach service from Wayzata to St. Paul via Minneapolis and St. Anthony. Trails, shaped by feet, horse, or beast-drawn cart or sleigh later became graded roads smoothed by horses dragging timbers. Lake waters offered year-round travel options, and vessels of all power sources evolved—row, sail, steam, and gas. Regardless of the season, travel across the water was often preferred to rutted, muddy trails on land.

The first locomotive in the lake area, *St. Cloud No. 7*, chugged into Wayzata in 1867, followed by railroad service to Excelsior in 1881, Spring Park in 1890, and Mound in 1900. Trains delivered materials and transported people to and from the lake area. Boats ferried supplies to build hotels and restaurants and the visitors to fill them. Tourism escalated, and with it came a rivalry for wealth and control. Businessmen James J. Hill from St. Paul and William Washburn from Minneapolis began what has been called the Seven Year War. From 1879 until 1886, both invested heavily, competing over rail, water, and land for the opportunity to squire visitors to numerous havens of rest and leisure. As transportation evolved, everyone benefited—commuter travel became efficient and affordable, and summer populations swelled, bringing prosperity and a recreational reputation to be envied.

The national railroad boom, and then automobiles, ushered in the lake's next transportation phases. Eastern tourists eyed the West, newly accessible by train, changing Lake Minnetonka into a local resort. The Twin City Rapid Transit Company began streetcar service from Minneapolis and St. Paul in 1905, adding matching express boats the following year. Improvements to roads and bridges encouraged year-round residency, while car and motorcycle clubs, bicycling, yachting, and ice boating became popular pastimes for both tourists and residents.

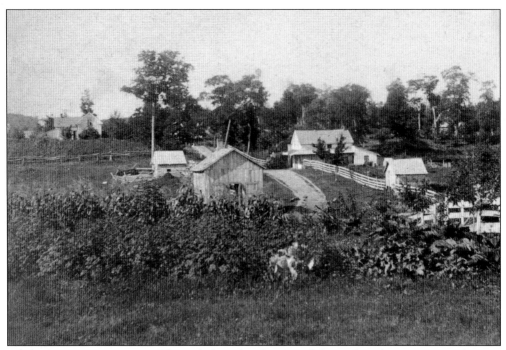

Early Excelsior, c. 1864. This is believed to be one of the earliest known views of Water Street, thought to have been taken from today's Lake and Water Streets looking southwest. The prominent structures pictured here are, from left to right, Horatio L. Beeman's house, Morris H. Pease's barn, David F. Henry's store, and Morris H. Pease's store. Water Street was named for a small stream that ran from Galpin Lake to Lake Minnetonka. (ELMHS.)

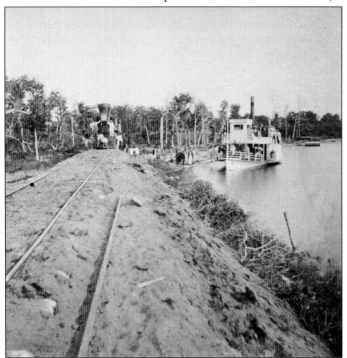

Rail and Steam Arrives. August 24, 1867, was a historic travel day on Lake Minnetonka, as the St. Paul and Pacific Railroad first arrived in Wayzata and was met by Charles Galpin's *Lady of the Lake* (previously the *Governor Ramsey*), the lake's first steamboat. The *St. Cloud No. 7* steam engine pulled one passenger car, reversed course on a turntable pulled by horses, and returned to St. Anthony. The *Lady* continued service until she was dismantled in 1874. (ELMHS.)

HULL'S NARROWS, TONKA BAY.
The shallow channel flowing through the marshes of wild rice connected the lake's upper and lower sections for boat travel. Named for 1853 settler Stephen Hull, it was dredged and border pilings were added in 1873. The new Narrows to the north was opened in 1884 and is still used. (ELMHS.)

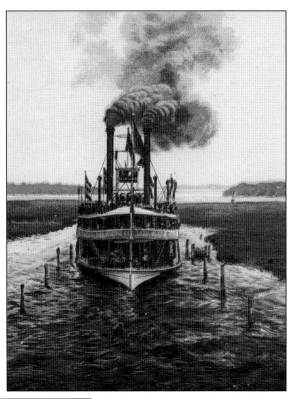

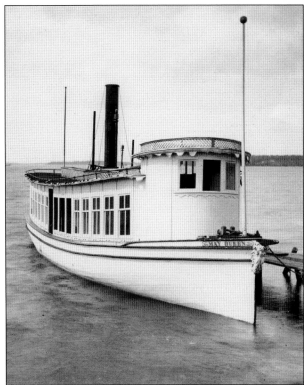

MAY QUEEN, C. 1876. Designed and built in 1874 by Capt. Nathaniel Harrison for Capt. Charles May, the *May Queen* was launched in Wayzata and operated by Capt. William Rockwell. It steamed around the lake, carrying up to 75 people, until exploding in 1879, injuring several passengers. Its boiler was manufactured by the same firm that supplied boilers to two other boats that met a similar end. (ELMHS.)

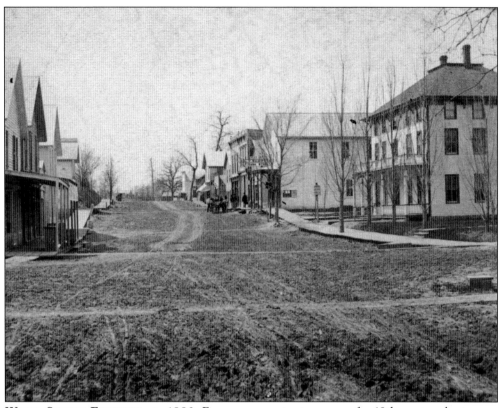

WATER STREET, EXCELSIOR, C. 1880. Fire was a constant concern for 19th-century businesses and homeowners. The Central Hotel (right), located at the corner of Water and Second Streets, burned to the ground on New Year's Eve 1894, along with nine blocks of Excelsior's downtown businesses and one private residence. This photograph looks southwest down Water Street from near Second Street. (ELMHS.)

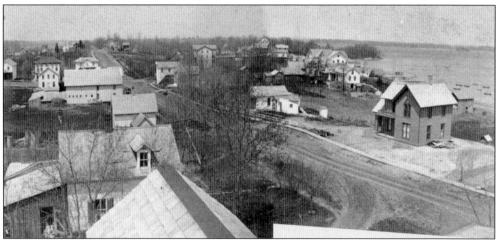

EXCELSIOR, C. 1883. This view from the roof of the Slater House looks northwest up Second Street toward Water Street from today's School Avenue. Major structures shown include, from left to right, the Central Boarding House, Dr. E.R. Perkins's home, Gates's Livery barn, Newell's store, Excelsior House (four stories), Long View House (three stories), and the White House hotel. (SDM.)

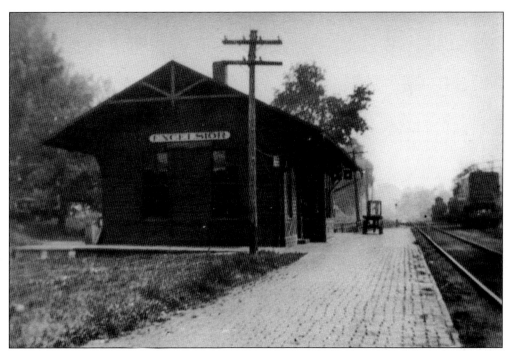

EXCELSIOR DEPOT. The Excelsior Depot stood at Water and Third Streets and was built by the Minneapolis and St. Louis Railway in 1883. The old station was demolished, and a new station was built in 1952 and continued to offer freight and passenger service. Passenger service stopped in 1960, and the building has housed the Excelsior–Lake Minnetonka Historical Society Museum since 1982. (Both, ELMHS.)

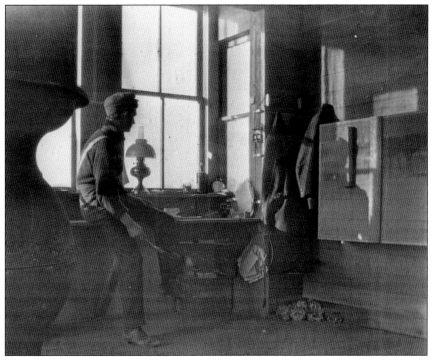

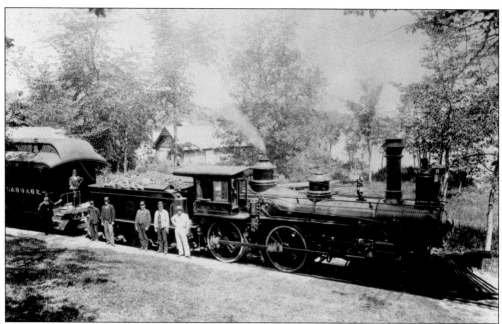

MINNEAPOLIS AND ST. LOUIS RAILWAY, LAKE PARK HOTEL, TONKA BAY, 1886. Once its tracks were laid to Excelsior in 1880–1881, the Minneapolis and St. Louis Railway ran 20 trains daily, bringing thousands from the Twin Cities to Lake Minnetonka's hotels, excursion boats, and attractions. Passenger service ended in 1960, and the tracks have been replaced by the Lake Minnetonka LRT Regional Trail. (ELMHS.)

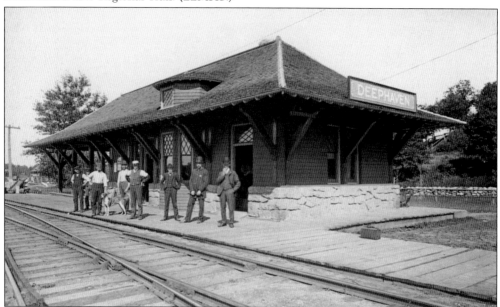

DEEPHAVEN DEPOT. The Minneapolis and St. Louis Railway depot was designed in 1891 by Hazen Burton, who built his home up the hill the next year and commuted to Minneapolis by train. Asked to name the depot, Burton's wife, Alice, chose Deephaven, the title of author Sarah Orne Jewett's collection of stories and sketches about a coastal village in Maine. Passenger service ended by 1937, and the depot is now a private residence in Cottagewood. (SDM.)

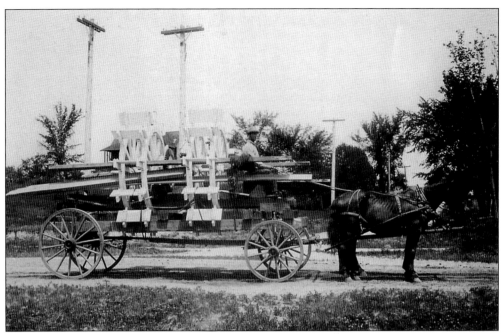

WAYZATA DELIVERY WAGON. Prior to 1900, horses and oxen were the animals of choice for transportation and work. The paddle wheels on this wagon may have just arrived by train and are probably on their way to one of the local boat builders in Wayzata. (WZHS.)

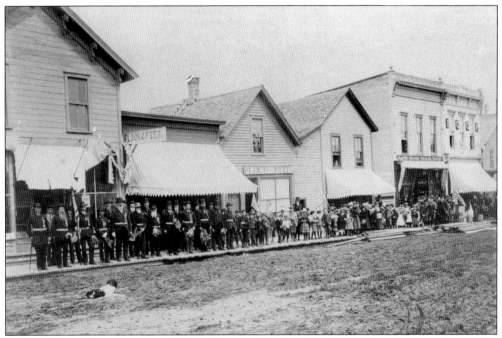

WATER STREET, EXCELSIOR, 1892. Grand Army of the Republic Civil War veterans gather on the west side of Water Street to commemorate Memorial Day. All the buildings behind them were destroyed by fire on New Year's Eve 1894. The IOOF Hall can be seen at far right. (ELMHS.)

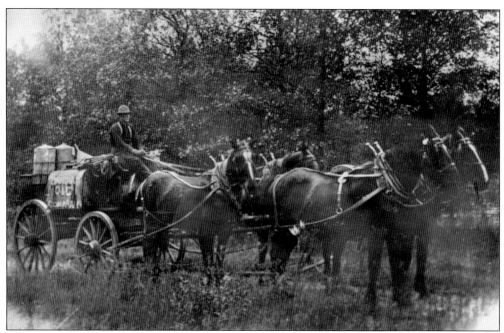

BENNETT STANDARD OIL DELIVERY RIG. Brothers Melvin and Harley Bennett founded the Excelsior livery in the 1890s. They expanded into almost every horse-drawn service available in the Lake Minnetonka area, from coal oil delivery to the transportation of headstones for graves and wood for caskets, finally cornering the market with their own custom-built hearse. (ELMHS.)

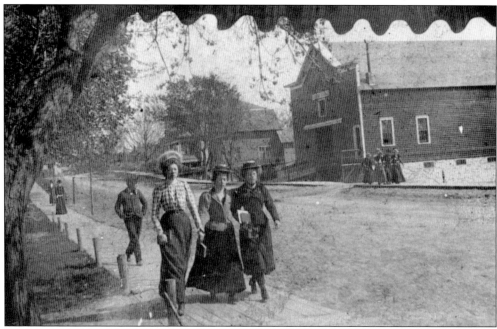

SECOND AND WATER STREETS, EXCELSIOR, EARLY 1900S. Strollers along Second Street are about to pass the photographer, whose camera is under the awning of the Minnetonka State Bank building. Across the street on the right is Bennett Brothers' Livery, built in 1900, which became an "auto livery" in 1910. Both the bank building and the former livery stand today. (ELMHS.)

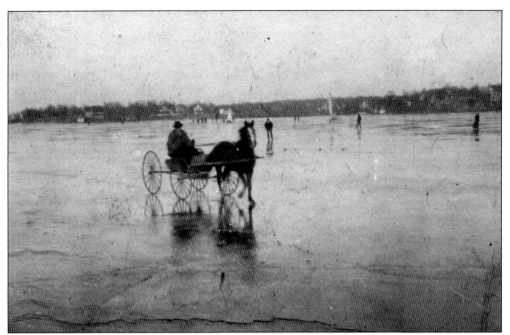

WINTER LAKE TRANSPORTATION. Skaters, pedestrians, and ice yachts join this horse and buggy traveling on the frozen lake. The first settlers waited for the lake to freeze, then traveled and moved their goods using the most direct route across the lake, plowing roads on the ice to facilitate travel. (ELMHS.)

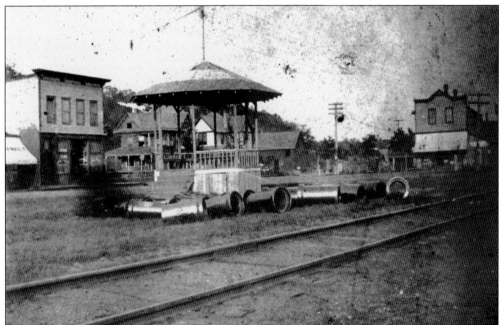

WAYZATA BAND SHELL. Beginning in the late 1880s, Wayzata had a band shell in the center of town at what is now Lake Street and Broadway Avenue. During summer months, the Cornet Band performed for villagers and tourists in matching uniforms. A modest structure, the band shell shook when the horns and snare drum were played. (WZHS.)

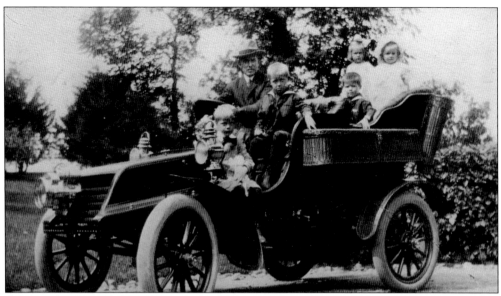

AUTOMOBILE TRAVEL. The Bovey family of Ferndale hopped aboard their 1901 Winton for car outings. The exterior basket held conveniences, and the wicker umbrella holder above the rear tire was a necessity for a car without a top. Passengers could enter and exit the vehicle through a rear door. (WZHS.)

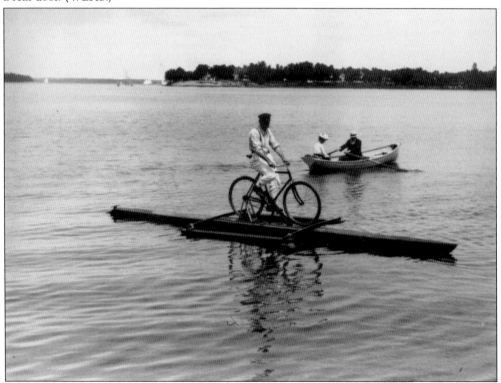

WATER BICYCLE, c. 1902. Excelsior boat builder Andrew Peterson is demonstrating his version of the "Bicycle Boat" or "Water Cycle," a popular novelty in the 1890s. When pedaled, a submerged wheel turned a propeller at the stern. (HCL.)

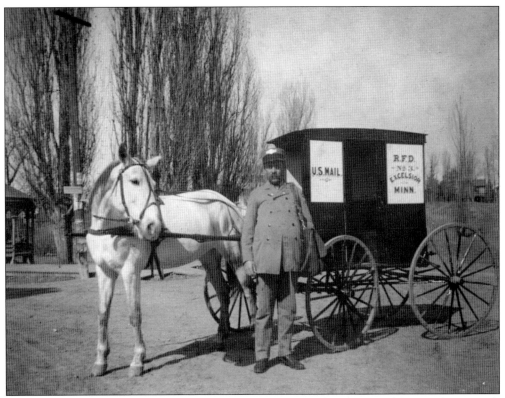

MAIL DELIVERY, EXCELSIOR, 1902. Excelsior was a hub for the new Rural Free Delivery, with routes radiating out from the town to farmlands. Lou Perkins began 35-mile rural route No. 3 in 1900 with his mare, Pet, who missed only 12 trips. He reported that the winter of 1904 was a strenuous one, but he had not missed a trip or frozen any part of his body. (ELMHS.)

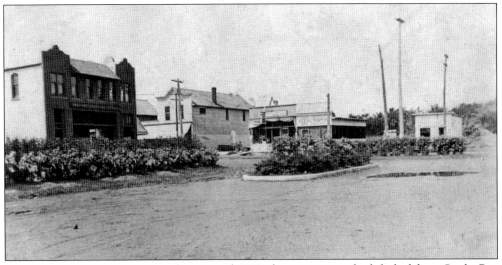

MOUND, 1905. Known as Mound City until 1912, the town center had shifted from Cooks Bay and Busy Corners north to Shoreline Drive and Commerce Boulevard (pictured). Originally cow paths, the roads intersected near the train depot where the hardware store, lumber yard, livery and taxi service, and dry goods store had been built. (WTHS.)

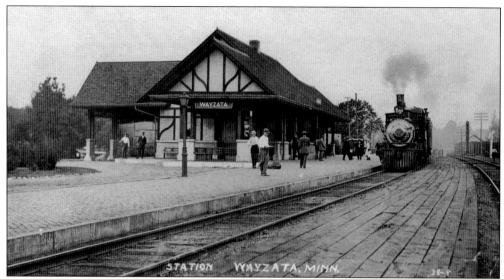

GREAT NORTHERN RAILROAD DEPOT, WAYZATA. This Tudor-style depot was designed by Samuel Bartlett for railroad president James J. Hill and completed in 1906. Considered the most handsome depot on the line, it had platform canopies, steam heat, gas lights, modern toilets, and drinking fountains. When passenger service was discontinued in 1971, it was donated to the city and today houses a museum operated by the Wayzata Historical Society. It is listed in the National Register of Historic Places. (WZHS.)

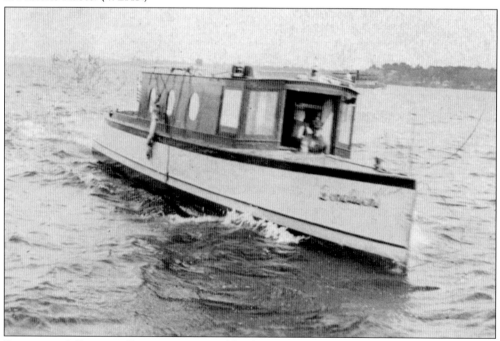

DONALDSON'S DELIVERY BOAT, 1910. Boats like the *Donaldson* proved a direct and reliable means of delivering goods, as early area roads were often washed out or did not yet exist to all parts of the lake. Minneapolis department stores Donaldson's and Dayton's catered to summer residents and hotel guests. Donaldson's advertised "Minnetonka Boat Express Delivery, purchases made up to 5 pm will be delivered the next day." (ELMHS.)

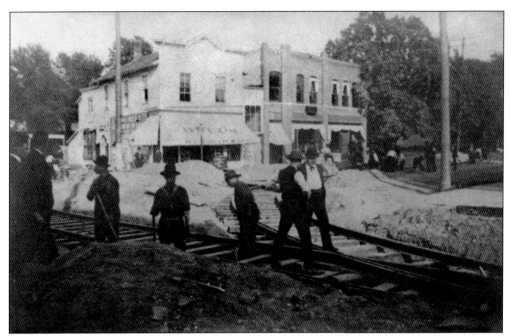

STREETCAR TRACKS AND STREETCAR, EXCELSIOR. The Twin Cities Rapid Transit Company extended its streetcar service to Excelsior in 1905, and workmen are pictured above laying track down Water and Second Streets. Double-decker cars lifted passengers out of the dust and smoke of the roadway and provided excellent views of the lake. The line was discontinued in 1932 when bus service began. (Above, ELMHS; below, HCL.)

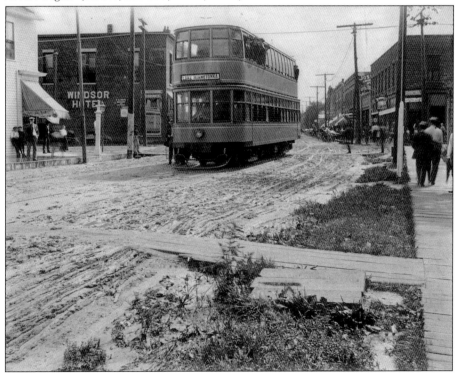

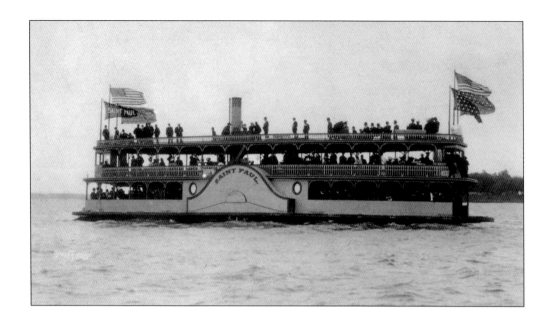

BIG ISLAND FERRY AND EXCELSIOR DOCKS, 1906. One of Lake Minnetonka's most popular, albeit short-lived, destinations was Big Island Amusement Park (1906–1911). A special ferry service, using vessels like the *Saint Paul* (above), was established between Excelsior and the park's docks. The Excelsior Ferry Docks (below) accommodated double-ended boats capable of steering from either end, with an employee stationed in the clock tower to coordinate their trips. The streetcar station can be seen behind the docks on the right. The streetcar line and matching express boats, docks, ferries, and amusement park were owned by Thomas Lowry's Twin Cities Rapid Transit Company. (Above, HCL; below, ELMHS.)

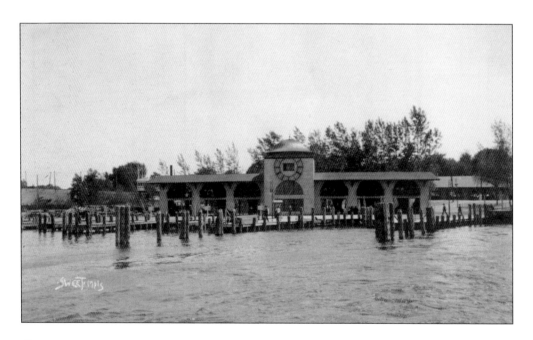

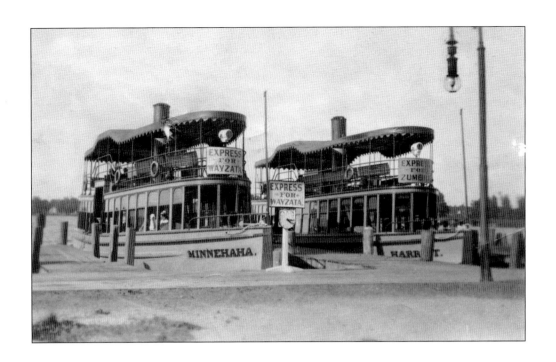

STREETCAR BOATS. The Twin City Rapid Transit Company added streetcar boat service to Lake Minnetonka in 1906. Wayzata resident Royal C. Moore designed six express boats to match their land-based counterparts. They were a popular fleet, meeting passengers at the streetcars and other locations and transporting them to scheduled stops around the lake. Service ended in 1926, and four boats were scuttled off Big Island. The *Minnehaha* was raised in 1980 and restored. Today, she is back on the lake, operated by the Museum of Lake Minnetonka. (Above, ELMHS; below, WTHS.)

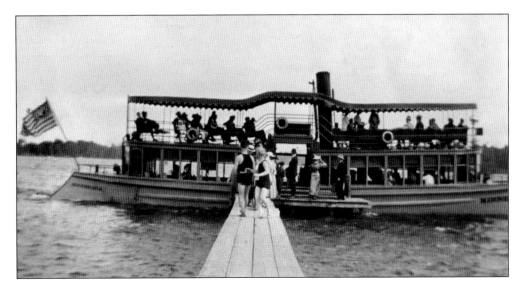

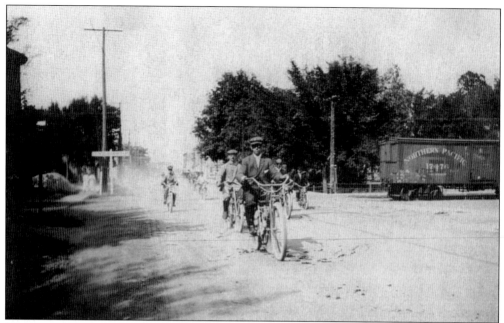

MINNEAPOLIS MOTORCYCLE CLUB, EXCELSIOR. Riding bicycles and motorcycles to Lake Minnetonka from the Twin Cities quickly became a popular summer pastime. The motorcyclists seen here in the early 1900s are heading southwest on Water Street, having just crossed the tracks near Third Street. (ELMHS.)

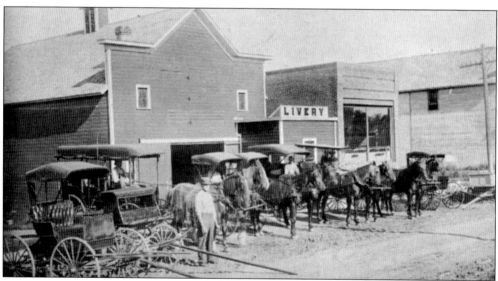

MOUND LIVERY. Located near Mound's Great Northern Railroad depot in 1910, William Krause greeted arriving train passengers with livery buses and drove them to their hotels and cottages. His brother Joseph owned the horses pulling the 10-seat taxis. In 1912, the brothers offered service with Ford cars, trucks, and buses, replacing them biannually due to poor road conditions that ruined tires and shook the vehicles apart. (ELMHS.)

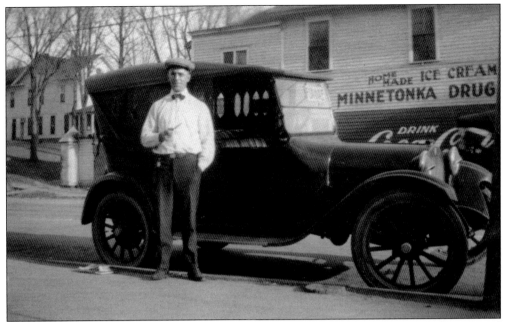

EXCELSIOR TAXICAB, 1912. Although the horse and buggy would give way to the internal combustion engine, the older terminology held sway for a time. Catering primarily to the hotel and tourist trade, fleets of early taxicabs, like the one seen here on Water and Second Streets, were known as auto livery. Pictured here in the background are Minnetonka Drug and the White House hotel. (ELMHS.)

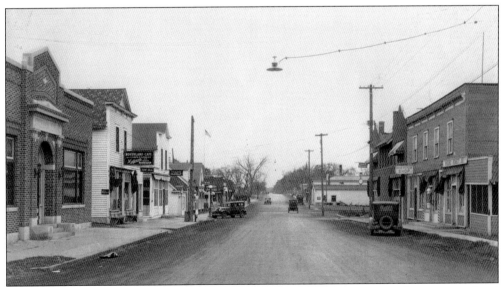

MOUND, C. 1912. In the newly incorporated town of Mound, tourists arriving by train stimulated business in the uptown commercial district surrounding the Great Northern Depot and at Busy Corners near Cooks Bay. Tourists filled the eight hotels, and residents supported initiatives for improved roads, sidewalks, and business opportunities. This view looks north on Commerce Boulevard. (WTHS.)

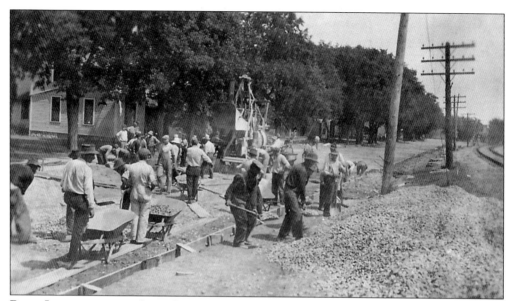

ROAD IMPROVEMENT ON LAKE STREET, WAYZATA, 1916. Property owners requested sidewalks in Wayzata, paying a 37.5¢-per-yard assessment, and they were installed in 1902. Road paving was not yet a city priority, as locals lived on rural farms or near their businesses and walked to work. As automobile ownership increased, paved roads became more common and were welcomed. (WZHS.)

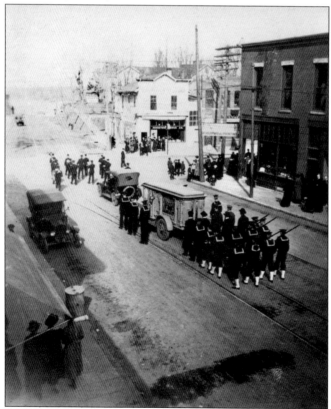

FUNERAL PROCESSION, WATER STREET, EXCELSIOR, 1919. Clarence Clofer, a popular Excelsior High School graduate, enlisted in the Navy when the United States entered World War I. He was killed in 1919 in an explosion aboard a submarine chaser off Key West, Florida. Although not killed in combat, his burial at Oak Hill Cemetery was afforded the equivalent of full military honors and the entire town closed from 2:30 p.m. to 5:00 p.m. to pay its respects. (ELMHS.)

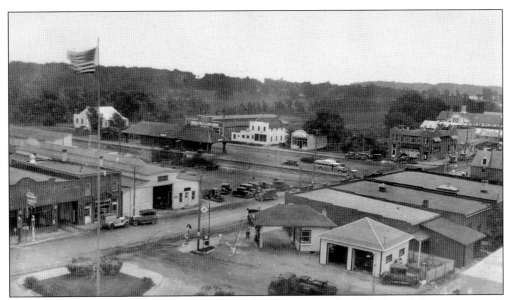

MOUND, C. 1920. Looking south on Commerce Boulevard are, clockwise from left, an auto repair shop, hardware and lumber yard, train depot, hotel, *Pilot* newspaper building, Longpre Block, Catholic church, Crocker Building with post office and grocer, and Herman Glewwe's Standard Oil station on the corner. The population included about 450 year-round residents, ballooning to 3,000 in the summer. (WTHS.)

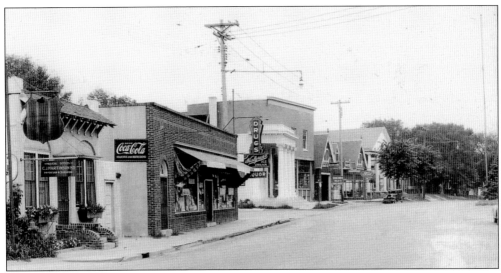

MARTINSON CORNER, WAYZATA. Looking east along Lake Street in the early 1930s were, from left to right, the C.J. Martinson clinic, Wayzata Pharmacy, Wayzata State Bank, Pettitt & Kysor Grocery, Rettinger Ford, and the village hall. All the buildings, except Rettinger Ford and the village hall, remain today. (WZHS.)

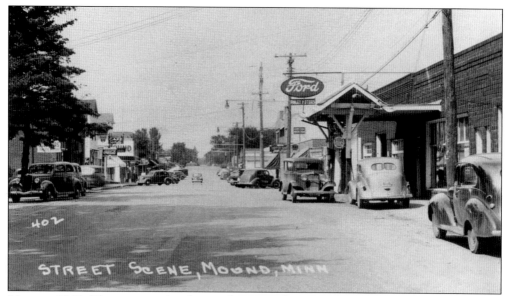

MOUND, 1942. The town was bustling with its paved streets, automobile traffic, and sidewalks to encourage strolling and window shopping. Finley Motors, Mound's first car dealership, is at right. At left are Yost Drugstore, the theater, and the bank. (WTHS.)

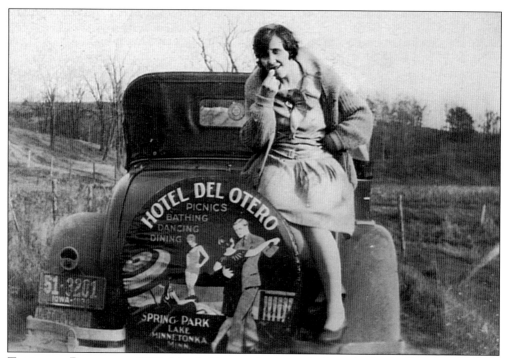

TRAVELING BILLBOARD, 1937. Myrtle Youngquist is perched on the back of a car sporting a tire cover advertising the Hotel Del Otero in Spring Park. Wherever Myrtle drove, others were reminded that the hotel was open for picnicking, dancing, and beach fun. (ELMHS.)

Four

THE LURE OF THE LAKE

Lake Minnetonka's first visitors and campers toured the lake by boat in 1852. In that year, writer Elizabeth Ellet explored the lake, describing "waters so clear we could often see the sandy bottom, and numbers of fish sporting round us; they had not learned to dread the angler!" Spirit Knob, considered sacred by the Indians and used as a ceremonial site, was a favorite attraction, followed by a stop at Big Island for picnickers to enjoy hiking through its wilderness. Private homes became boardinghouses and later hotels. In 1879, both the Lake Park and Hotel St. Louis were built, attracting tourists from the South and East seeking the luxuries they were accustomed to elsewhere. Opulent hotels and steamboats were seasonal ventures, beginning in June and ending in September.

Shipwrights built excursion boats like the *Mary* for Frank Halsted, stern-wheelers like the *Hattie May*, and steamboats *Belle of Minnetonka* and the *City of Saint Louis*, built in Wayzata boatyards. Within a decade, thousands had registered in newly built hotels, and they told their friends. *The Northwestern Tourist* gushed over the cool breezes and clean air—a place to recover or gain respite from ailments of the body and spirit. Visitors rented boats of every kind. They camped and they celebrated, listening to orchestras serenading them into the night. Lake Minnetonka was a resort destination rivaling any Eastern counterpart and beckoned everyone to share her waters.

As Lake Minnetonka's national tourism boom faded and people headed for more distant attractions, the lake remained a destination for local tourists and year-round residents. Sailing, fishing, and swimming continued to be popular. Twin Cities companies and civic groups patronized local parks, assembly grounds, and amusement parks for picnics and outdoor recreation. The lure of the lake and its history continue to draw visitors to its shores today.

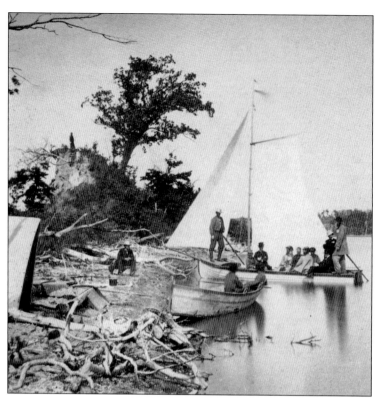

SPIRIT KNOB, WOODLAND, 1860s. Known as one of the oldest landmarks on the lake and a popular tourist destination, Spirit Knob was once a knob-shaped bluff at the end of Breezy Point. Approximately 50 feet high with a lone tree at the top, it was used as a sacred ceremonial ground by Indians. Over time it eroded, and it was leveled due to safety concerns in 1885. (ELMHS.)

NEWARK HOUSE, MINNETONKA MILLS. This was the second hotel built in the first settlement near Lake Minnetonka. Known as the Jackson Hotel in 1857, by 1873 it had grown to 18 rooms. The hotel also housed mill workers and later served as a boardinghouse until 1892. It was located across from the old town hall on Baker Road and is no longer standing. (HHM.)

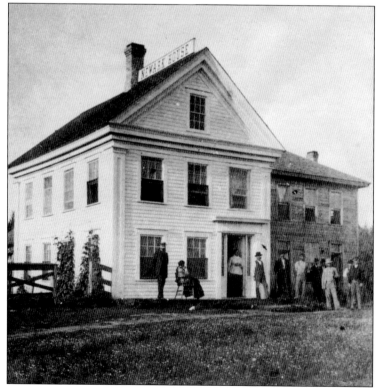

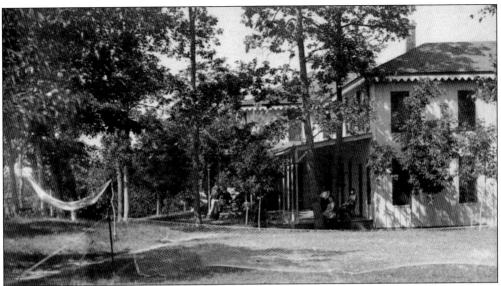

MAPLEWOOD INN, WOODLAND. Built by Samuel Gale in 1868 on a hill south of Breezy Point, this was thought to be the first summer cottage on the lake. It became a boardinghouse and was enlarged to 20 guest rooms. Later a hotel with a lakeside pavilion, it burned in 1903, but the laundry shed survived and was used as a school in September and May for cottagers' children. (ELMHS.)

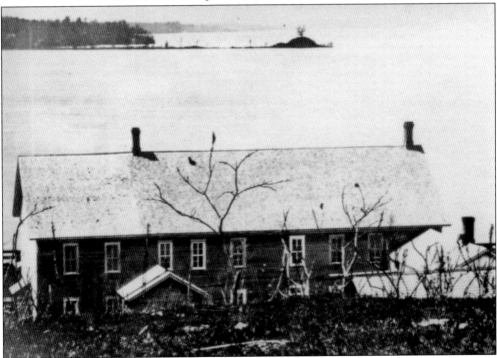

MINNETONKA HOUSE, WAYZATA. Built in 1870 by Henry Maurer and William Rockwell, this hotel along Lake Street overlooked Wayzata Bay with a view of Spirit Knob. Renamed the Minnetonka House by 1876, it had a billiard hall, a "blind pig" in the basement, and housed 100 guests, including James Gang members en route to rob the First National Bank of Northfield, Minnesota. (ELMHS.)

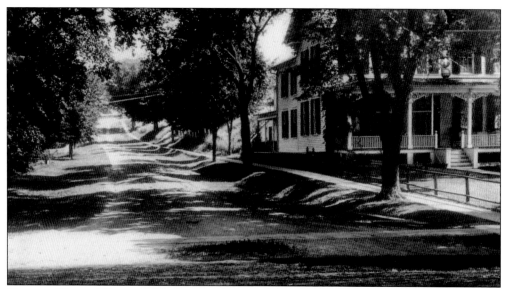

GLEASON HOUSE, WAYZATA. The last hotel to stand in Wayzata was built in 1867 as the Mattison House on what is now Lake Street and Walker Avenue. It was purchased by Horace Gleason in 1870 and expanded to house 40 guests. It included a boathouse and was popular with families who paid $14 weekly, including meals. It was still operated by Gleason family members in the 1880s and was an apartment building in 1938 before being razed in 1966. (WZHS.)

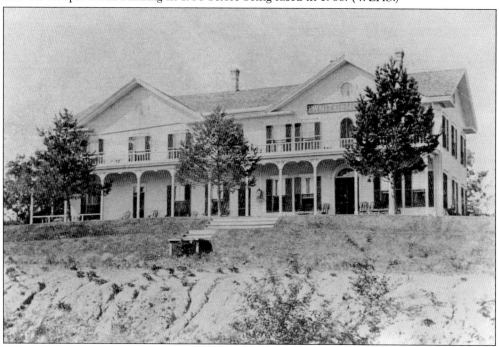

WHITE HOUSE, EXCELSIOR, c. 1880s. A hostelry stood on this hill at Water and Lake Streets beginning in 1855. Known as the White House by 1879, the hotel was expanded and eventually accommodated 200 guests. The Woman's Club of Lake Minnetonka operated it in 1921, incorporating their community house and a public library. In 1929, it became the Minnesota State Sunshine Society home for the aged. In 1946, it was demolished and the hill was leveled. (ELMHS.)

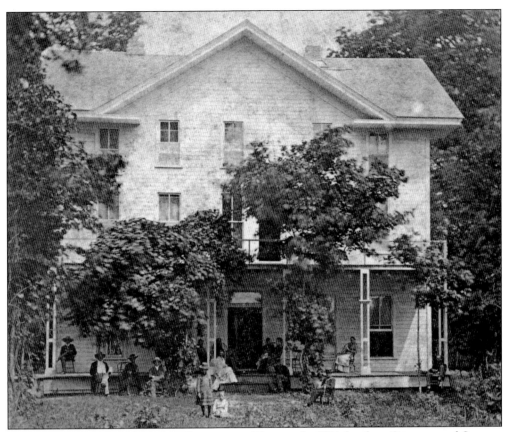

CHAPMAN HOUSE AND CHAPMAN BOATHOUSE, MOUND. In 1876, brothers Seymour and Sumner Chapman built this lakeside hotel on Cooks Bay (pictured above around 1880), and after a booming first season, the hotel was doubled in size. In 1886, John Chapman and Frank Carman purchased the complex. The hotel survived fire damage in 1892, resulting in remodeling and a new boathouse. By 1890, Chapman was the sole proprietor and added a waterside casino. The casino and boathouse burned after 1916. Both were rebuilt, and the hotel continued into the 1930s. The casino became the Surfside Restaurant until the building was razed in 1986. (Above, SDM; below, WTHS.)

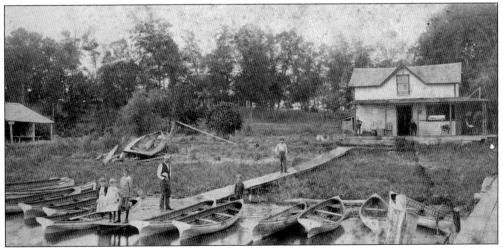

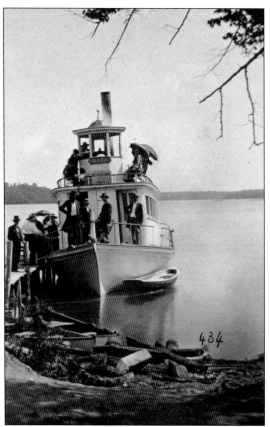

THE MARY. Built in 1876 for Capt. Frank Halsted, the *Mary* was named for his mother. After Frank's death in 1876, his brother Maj. George Halsted inherited the vessel and transported tourists around the lake. In 1880, her boiler exploded, injuring eight people and killing four; Halsted was indicted for criminal negligence. The *Mary* was rebuilt and launched in 1881 as the *Hiawatha*, then moved to Green Lake, Minnesota, in 1887. (ELMHS.)

HATTIE MAY, C. 1880. Built in Excelsior for $10,000 and launched in 1878, the *Hattie May* was the first stern-wheel steamer on Lake Minnetonka. She was 100 feet long and could carry 350 to 500 passengers. Her interior featured an organ, Brussels carpet, and upholstered seats. She was docked from 1892 to 1896 due to poor business, rebuilt and renamed the *Tonka* in 1897, and caught fire and burned in 1900. (ELMHS.)

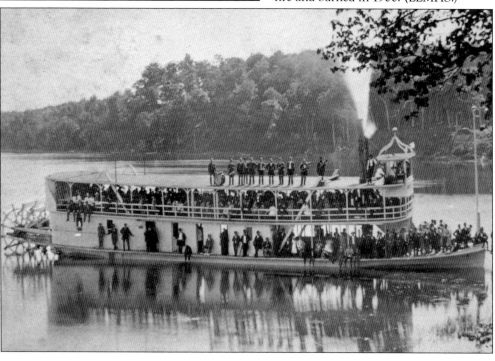

HOTEL ST. LOUIS, DEEPHAVEN. Built as the Hotel Harrow above St. Louis Bay in 1879, this was briefly the largest hotel on the lake, with 200 gas-lit rooms, a bath on every floor, and "plumbing of the highest quality." Served by two train lines, it was funded by and catered to Southerners escaping the heat. It was demolished in 1907 following a decade of poor business. (ELMHS.)

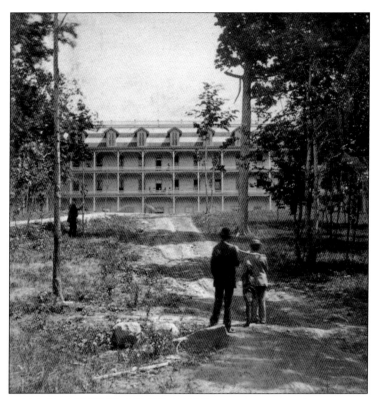

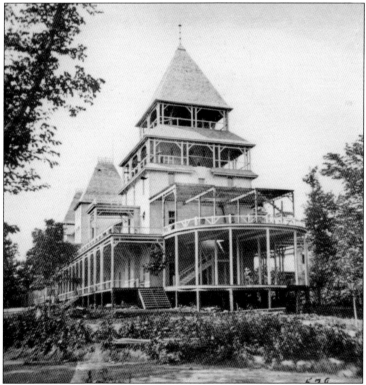

LAKE PARK HOTEL UNDER CONSTRUCTION, TONKA BAY, 1879. The Northwestern Sunday School Association built this hotel on a 250-acre peninsula on the Lower Lake. It was designed by Leroy Buffington as one of the lake's largest hotels, with accommodations for 500 guests plus a theater, ballroom, roller rink, and miles of shoreline. Remodeled and renamed the Tonka Bay Hotel in 1902, it was razed in 1913. (ELMHS.)

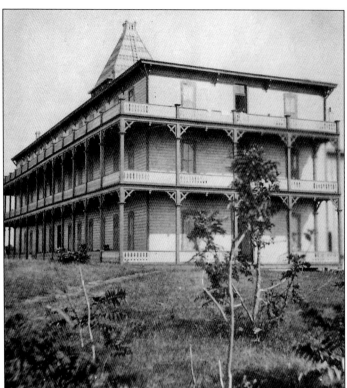

ARLINGTON HOTEL, WAYZATA. Built in 1880 by George Hyser and William Bowen for $25,000, including fixtures and furniture, this hotel stood near today's Shady Lane. It was the largest hotel in Wayzata, housing 150 guests with a grand dining room, 16-foot ceilings, and electric bells in each room. Vacant by 1882, the hotel was destroyed by fire in 1890. (WZHS.)

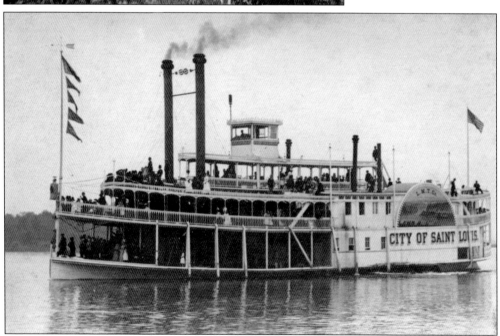

CITY OF SAINT LOUIS, C. 1883. This first large steamboat on the lake was built in 1881 for Sen. William D. Washburn. With room for 1,000 and dining for 500, she met trains in Wayzata and Excelsior. She was 160 feet long, 48 feet wide, and the first inland vessel in the country with electric lights. Dismantled in 1898, her remains were used for a dredging scow and party barge. (ELMHS.)

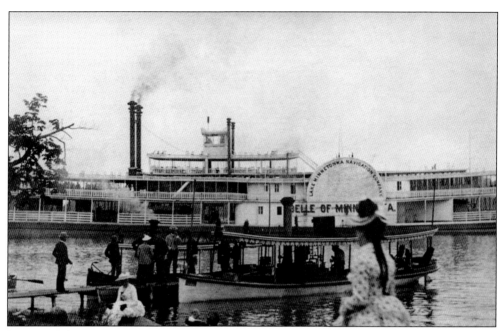

BELLE OF MINNETONKA, C. 1882. James J. Hill's *Belle* began as the riverboat *Phil Sheridan*. She was dismantled in Wisconsin and reassembled in Wayzata in 1882. At 300 feet long and 56 feet wide, she became the largest boat on the lake, carrying 2,500 passengers with several dining rooms, 40 sleeping berths, two orchestras, and electric lights. She was used infrequently after 1885 and scrapped in 1897. Her whistle was installed in the *City of Saint Louis*, and her bell is still in Excelsior. (ELMHS.)

WAYZATA WATERFRONT, 1881. At this busy port at the foot of Broadway Avenue South are passenger boats *Hattie May*, *City of Minneapolis*, *Lotus*, and *City of Saint Louis*. The small building on the dock rented boats and fishing gear to tourists. The railroad tracks were laid in 1867, and trains continue to travel through Wayzata today. (WZHS.)

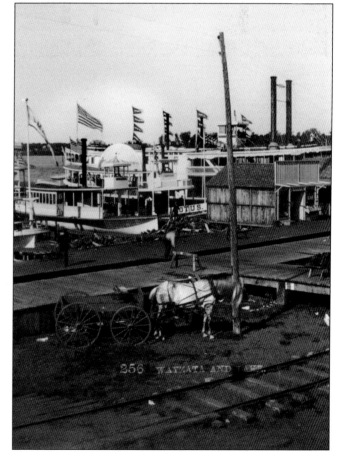

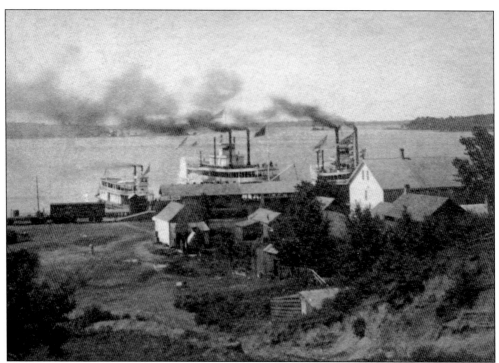

WAYZATA WATERFRONT, 1882. This photograph looks south down today's Broadway Avenue from Rice Street. The long building is the town's train station with waiting platform at right. At dock are excursion boats *Hattie May*, *Belle of Minnetonka*, and *City of Saint Louis*. The Minnetonka House stands at right. (ELMHS.)

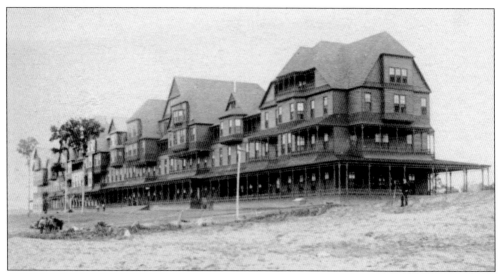

THE HOTEL LAFAYETTE UNDER CONSTRUCTION, MINNETONKA BEACH. Built in 1882 by James J. Hill to attract riders to his railroad, this summer hotel was the largest on the lake and considered one of the finest in the West. It overlooked Lafayette and Crystal Bays, and at 90 feet tall and 745 feet long, it had 300 rooms with every modern convenience. When fire destroyed the hotel in 1897, Hill sold the property to the founders of what would become the Lafayette Club. (ELMHS.)

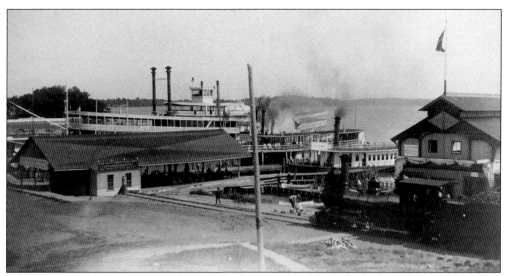

EXCELSIOR DOCKS, C. 1887. Seen at the docks are, from left to right, the *Belle of Minnetonka*, Gates & Dunlap Pavilion, the *Hattie May*, the *Clyde*, a steam locomotive, and the Minneapolis, Lyndale & Minnetonka Motor Line Pavilion. The motor line made up to six trips daily from Lake Harriet to Excelsior from 1882 to 1887. (ELMHS.)

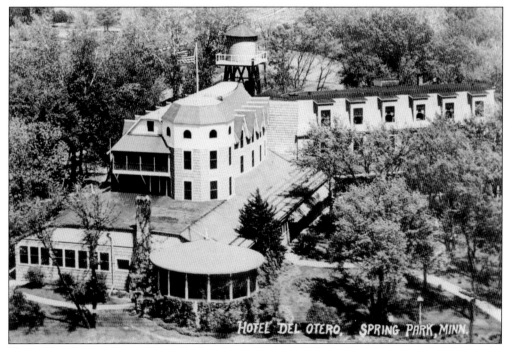

HOTEL DEL OTERO, SPRING PARK. Railroad mogul James J. Hill's St. Paul, Minneapolis & Manitoba Railway reached Spring Park in 1881, and this hotel was built in 1892. Accommodations included 50 guest rooms, the finest cuisine, and lake view acreage for strolling and picnicking. It was destroyed by fire in 1945. (WTHS.)

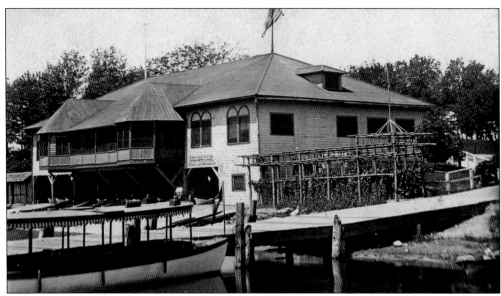

Spring Park Pavilion. Used for dances, boat rentals, and dining, few buildings on the lake have had the bad luck of this pavilion. It stood along Spring Park Bay on Shoreline Drive and was built by 1898, improved in 1900, destroyed by fire in 1902, rebuilt in 1903, damaged by a tornado in 1904, rebuilt in 1905, destroyed by fire in 1916, repaired again in 1925, and finally demolished after 1945. (WTHS.)

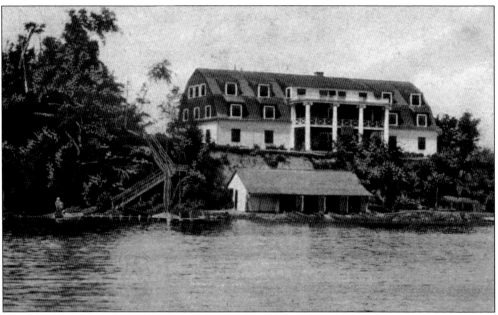

Maple Heights Inn, Phelps Island. James and Amanda Woolnough opened their hotel in 1891 and renovated it in 1903. Cottages were rented for $1.50 daily or $10 weekly. Located half a mile from the train in Spring Park, guests came by horse-drawn taxi and later on the streetcar boats directly to the island hotel. Demolished in 1964, it was the last summer hotel on the Upper Lake. (WTHS.)

PALMER HOUSE, ZUMBRA HEIGHTS. In 1887, John and Nellie Palmer opened their hotel atop the highest elevation in the lake area, overlooking Lakes Zumbra and Minnetonka. Promoted as a sanitarium for its cool breezes and endorsed by physicians for recuperation from insomnia and hay fever, the hotel was also popular as a sportsmen's resort. Nellie Palmer greeted guests arriving on the steamer *Mayflower* until she sold the hotel to Calvin Goodrich in 1904. (ELMHS.)

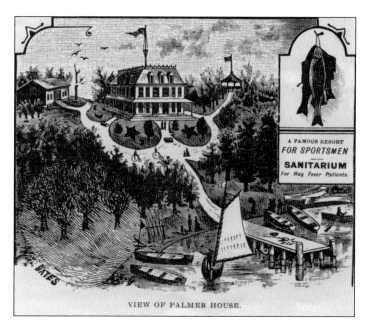

VIEW OF PALMER HOUSE.

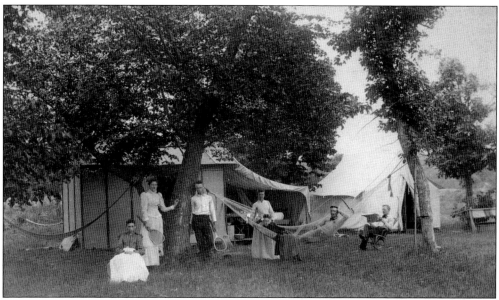

BAKER, PEASE, AND HASELTINE FAMILIES CAMPING AT ROBINSONS BAY, DEEPHAVEN, 1891. City folk, cottagers, and hotel guests camped during summer months in tents and hammocks cooled by lakeside breezes. They enjoyed water activities, dined al fresco on fresh-caught fish, or splurged on a hotel meal. Camping spots sported names like Camp Uneeda Rest and Mosquito Roost. Affordable lake vacations were attractive, and the *Minneapolis Tribune* reminded readers "it costs little to vegetate." (ELMHS.)

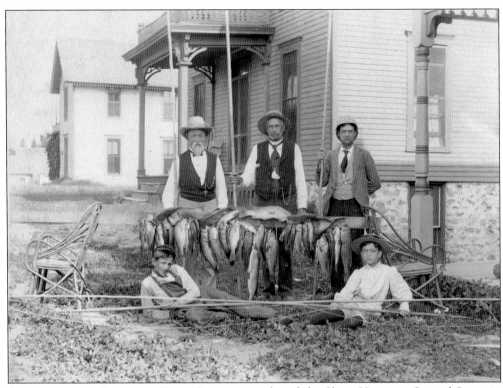

Sampson House, Excelsior. Laroy Sampson purchased the Slater House on Second Street in 1885 and renamed it. It featured over 40 rooms and was one of the few year-round hotels in the area. Although not on the lake, the hotel catered to fishermen, providing guides, boats, and gear with "full assurance of good strings of piscatorial beauties." After burning in 1893, it was rebuilt in 1895, and the Sampson family continued management until 1961 when the last large hotel on Lake Minnetonka was razed. (ELMHS.)

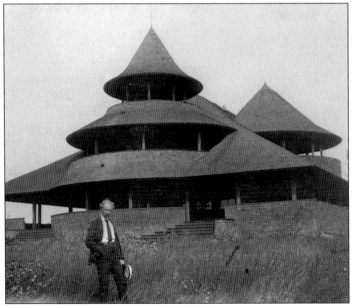

Minnetonka Yacht Clubhouse. Designed by Harry Wild Jones (pictured) in 1890, this clubhouse was built on Lighthouse Island in St. Louis Bay. The Shingle-style design had multilevel roof lines resembling full sails on the water. Following the landmark's opening were summer weekend picnics, Sunday concerts, and sailing races for the next 53 years. After surviving a fire in 1921, the clubhouse burned to the ground in 1943. (EV.)

MINNETONKA YACHT CLUB SAILORS, C. 1896.
The first Minnetonka Yacht Club regatta was held in 1882, followed by a regatta sponsored by the Excelsior Yacht Club the next year. Spectators watched the races from steamboats, launches, and other watercraft. Clubs today observe many of the same postrace traditions, including sharing food and drink. (HCL.)

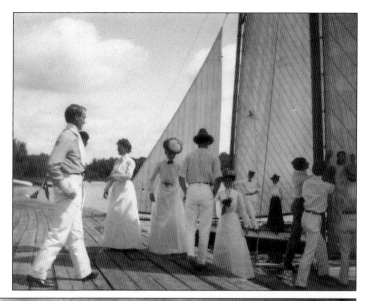

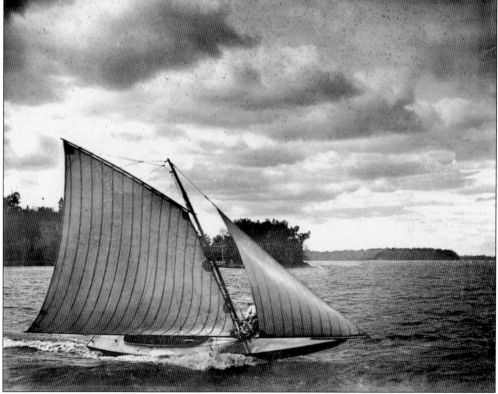

THE ONAWA, 1894. Built in 1893 by Arthur Dyer for Hazen and Ward Burton, the *Onawa's* design changed modern sailing. Weighing 500 pounds and carrying 400 square feet of sail, the 26-foot shallow-draught sloop was six feet four inches wide, flat ribbed, canvas covered, and had no ballast. She glided over the water like a canoe, averaging one minute per mile faster than any boat, and winning every race in 1893. Today, the *Onawa* is in the Excelsior–Lake Minnetonka Historical Society Museum. (ELMHS.)

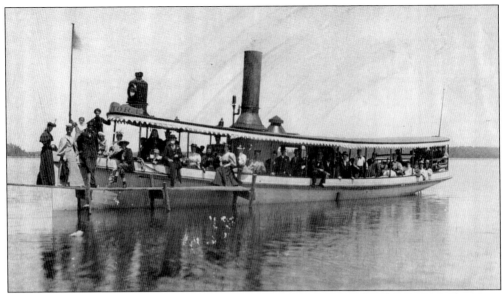

THE VICTOR, 1895. Built by Wayzata's Royal C. Moore as the *Kenozha*, this excursion boat was purchased by Capt. Theodore Champion in 1895 and renamed. In 1905, a new whistle gave the *Victor* a unique and recognizable sound. Unpopular, the whistle was short lived and quickly changed. Sold to Capt. George Hopkins in 1906, the *Victor* was dismantled in the fall of 1927. (WZHS.)

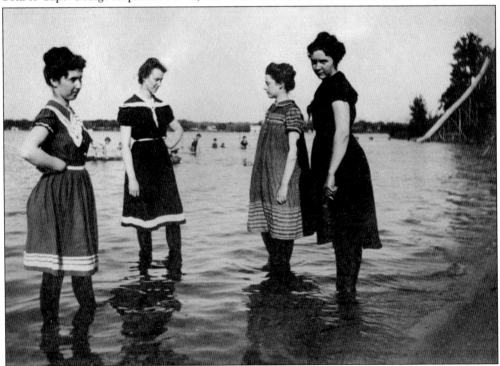

BATHERS, EXCELSIOR BEACH, 1902. Excelsior maintained a public beach beginning in 1876. Bathers enjoyed a 16-foot high-diving tower, a 50-foot toboggan chute or water slide (upper right), rolling logs for non-swimmers' entertainment, and different bathhouses over the years. Although the structures are now gone, the beach continues to be operated by the city. (ELMHS.)

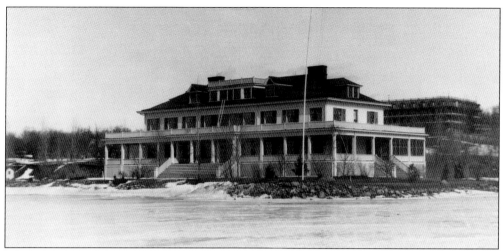

MINNETONKA ICE YACHT CLUBHOUSE, CARSONS BAY; ICE YACHT RACING, DEEPHAVEN. In 1900, Ice Yacht Club founder Theodore Wetmore donated this clubhouse on Bug Island in front of the Hotel St. Louis (above). By 1901, 167 members had 17 boats with more on the way. That same year, Ward Burton, the first ice racer on Lake Minnetonka, sailed the five miles from Gideon Bay to Wayzata on his boat *Zero* in three minutes and 45 seconds—105 mph—the fastest man had ever traveled. Burton remarked in his memoirs that "White sails passing over blue ice under a blue sky gave the illusion of flight." In 1904, the clubhouse was destroyed by fire. It was said to have been built by Syd Woodford, "who would build beautiful houses, docks and peanut stands with equal facility." (Above, HCL; below, ELMHS.)

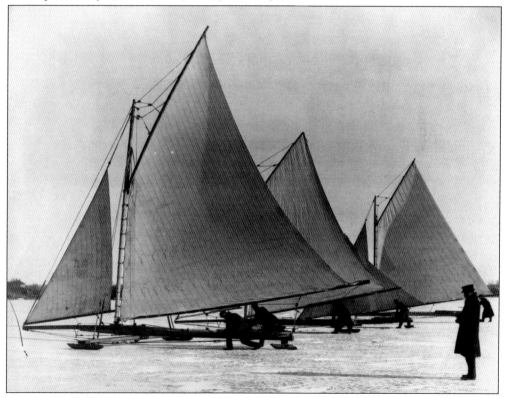

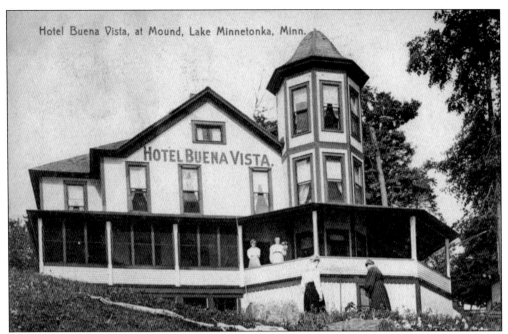

HOTEL BUENA VISTA, MOUND. Julia Butterfield opened the Buena Vista in 1901, and Capt. Jack Hart joined the hotel management in 1902. Located on the western highlands of Cooks Bay, guests came by train and then by streetcar, boat, and car, looking for a restful experience and to fish, as Hart was known as the "dean of Minnetonka fishermen." The hotel closed in 1919 and burned down in 1923. (WTHS.)

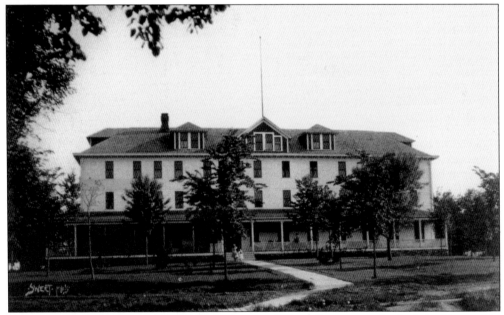

HOTEL KEEWAYDIN, DEEPHAVEN. Built on the site of Hotel Cottagewood, which had burned in 1902, the Keewaydin opened in 1903, and within two years it had 75 rooms, a ballroom, restaurant, billiard room, and grounds for tennis and croquet. It was accessible by boat and train, with streetcar boats making scheduled stops at the dock. It burned in 1924. (ELMHS.)

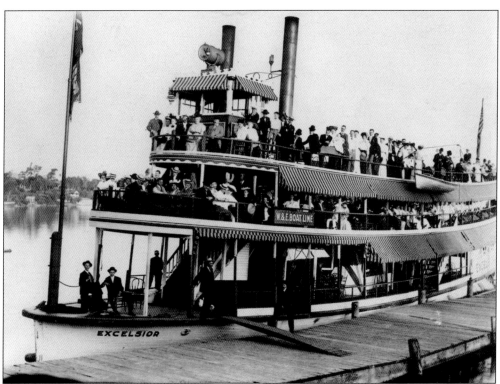

THE *EXCELSIOR*, C. **1905.** In 1901, Dr. George LaPaul built the *George*, spending $10,000 and launching her from the Excelsior docks before a crowd of 1,000 spectators. She held 800 passengers, was 125 feet long with a 22-foot beam, and reigned as the largest boat on the lake at the time. In 1904, she was remodeled with a full restaurant and rechristened the *Excelsior*. The Twin City Rapid Transit Company bought the boat for $3,250 in 1906 to reduce the competition for their streetcar boats, and she was considered antiquated and decommissioned two years later. In 1909, the *Excelsior* was stripped and set ablaze on the lake. Five thousand onlookers paid to take the Twin City Rapid Transit Company's streetcar to watch her burn to the waterline. (Both, ELMHS.)

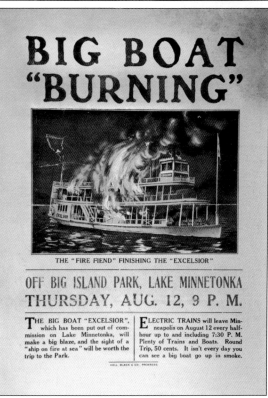

BIG BOAT "BURNING"

THE "FIRE FIEND" FINISHING THE "EXCELSIOR"

OFF BIG ISLAND PARK, LAKE MINNETONKA

THURSDAY, AUG. 12, 9 P. M.

THE BIG BOAT "EXCELSIOR", which has been put out of commission on Lake Minnetonka, will make a big blaze, and the sight of a "ship on fire at sea" will be worth the trip to the Park.

ELECTRIC TRAINS will leave Minneapolis on August 12 every half-hour up to and including 7:30 P. M. Plenty of Trains and Boats. Round Trip, 50 cents. It isn't every day you can see a big boat go up in smoke.

HALL, BLACK & CO. PRINTERS

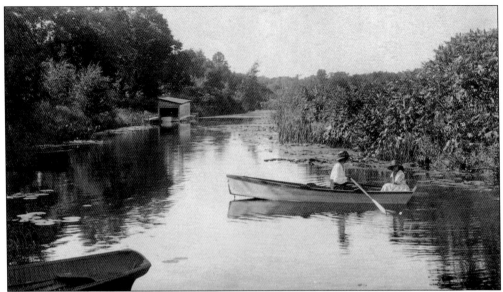

HARRISONS BAY, C. 1906. In 1855, Capt. Nathaniel Harrison purchased property on the north shoreline of Lake Minnetonka, along the bay that would be named for him. A shipwright originally from Virginia, Harrison built boats on the lake from 1874 until 1880, including steamers *Mary, May Queen,* and the *City of Minneapolis.* (WTHS.)

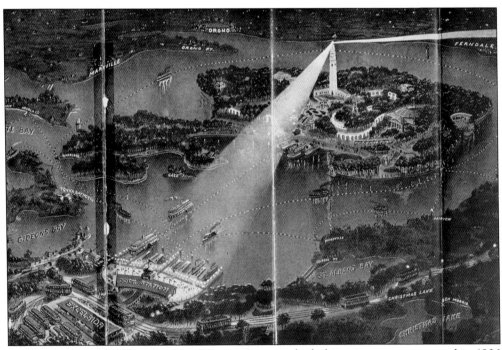

BIG ISLAND PARK. The Twin City Rapid Transit Company built this unique amusement park in 1906 as a destination for their streetcar riders. Passengers could ride from the Twin Cities, connect with special ferries at the lake, and enjoy 65 landscaped acres, well equipped picnic kitchens, concerts, rides, and a 200-foot electric tower powered by an underwater cable from the mainland. Too expensive to operate seasonally, the park was closed in 1911 and was demolished. (ELMHS.)

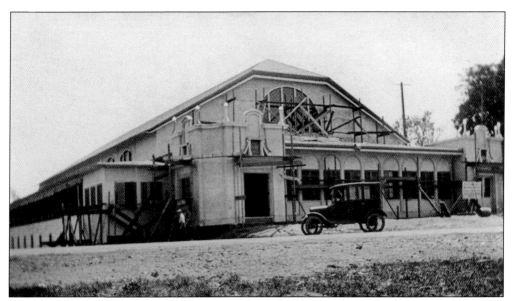

DANCELAND BEING REASSEMBLED, EXCELSIOR, 1923. Built as the Tonka Bay Casino in 1904, it was disassembled, brought to Excelsior, and rebuilt in 1922–1923 near Excelsior Bay. It was purchased by the Excelsior Amusement Park in 1929 and included a 70-by-150-foot dance floor that could accommodate 2,000 dancers. Entertainers included Lawrence Welk, the Beach Boys in 1963, and the Rolling Stones in 1964. Known later as Big Reggie's Danceland, it closed in 1968 and was used as a boat storage warehouse until destroyed by arson in 1973. (HHM.)

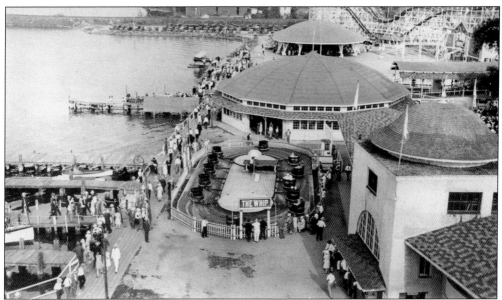

EXCELSIOR AMUSEMENT PARK. Sited on Excelsior Bay, this park was opened in 1925 by Fred Pearce. It cost $250,000 to build and included a roller coaster, a carousel with hand-carved horses, a fun house, a Ferris wheel, bumper cars, and a miniature train. Its annual Fourth of July fireworks were a tradition. The park was dismantled in 1974, but its carousel and Scrambler are still in service at Valleyfair in Shakopee, Minnesota. (ELMHS.)

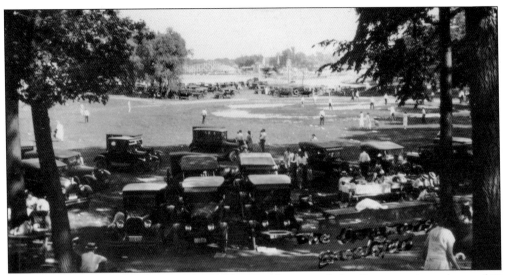

EXCELSIOR COMMONS, 1926. Platted in 1854 as public ground, the Commons is made up of 17 acres of lakeside property. Over the years, it has been home to bathhouses, pavilions, boat works, yacht clubs, playgrounds, picnic areas, baseball fields, tennis courts, and a band shell. It has hosted thousands for church, family, and company picnics, as well as camping and community celebrations like fireworks on the Fourth of July. (ELMHS.)

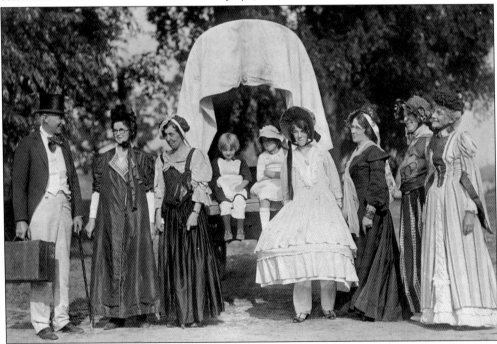

EXCELSIOR PAGEANT, 1926. Community pageants have been held in the Excelsior Commons at least five times since 1916. Pictured here, *The Pageant of Minnetonka*, by local newspaper editor Willard Dillman, presented the history of the area with some of the actors portraying their ancestors. It included 800 amateur local actors, 100 horses, livestock, and musicians, with thousands in the audience surrounded by the natural lake setting. Tickets were 25¢, and proceeds benefited community causes. (ELMHS.)

ELIZABETH LYMAN LODGE, GREENWOOD. In 1918, Frederick Lyman donated his summer estate to the YWCA, which used it as a summer camp and named it in honor of his late wife. Girls from around the state visited each summer to sail, canoe, camp, play tennis, swim, trail ride, and enjoy arts and crafts. From 1973 to 1990, the camp became a retreat center and was then sold. The lodge was demolished, and the property was subdivided. (ELMHS.)

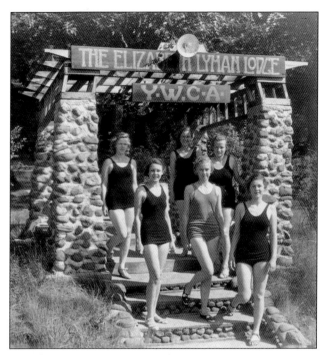

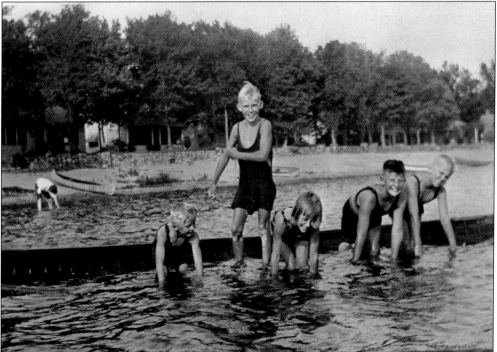

DOUGLAS BEACH, PHELPS ISLAND, 1919. Youngsters of summer cottagers pose on Douglas Beach on the southern tip of the island. In 1910, the Tuxedo Park Company of Minneapolis began selling island lots, advertising the area as a "delightful summer playground." Neighborhoods were given English names like Chester, Pembroke, and Avalon, and they had docks and regular boat service to the Spring Park train station. (WTHS.)

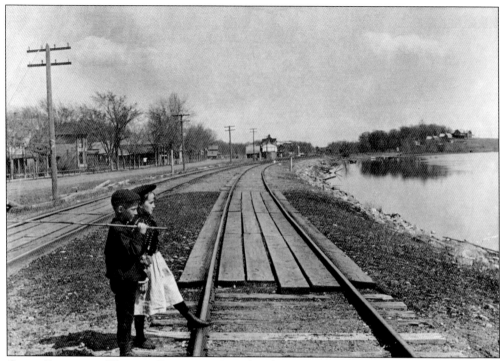

GOING FISHING ON WAYZATA BAY, C. 1895. In this sleepy town of fewer than 300 residents, these children did not have far to walk from Lake Street to Wayzata Bay for an afternoon of fishing. The original two sets of railroad tracks can be seen winding east along Lake Street. Today, the view of the bay remains unchanged, with businesses and residences located along the north side of the street. (ELMHS.)

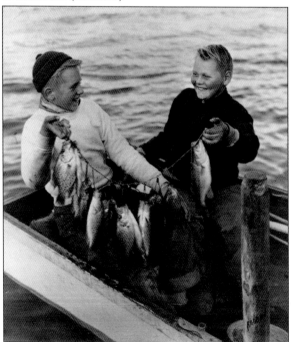

FISHING AT MAXWELL BAY, C. 1953. Brothers Jerry (left) and Tom Rockvam are all smiles fishing at Roxy's, their parents' resort. According to a 1949 survey, about one million pounds of fish were in the lake. Northern pike, black crappies, and walleyes were common in northern bays, perch could be found in Halsted Bay, and bluegills swam in the shallow waters. (TR.)

Five

CULTIVATING COMMERCE AND COMMUNITY LIFE

Many Lake Minnetonka settlers farmed to feed their families, selling and trading their surplus. Village dwellers opened stores, businesses, and services to fill needs, and summer coffers swelled with tourist income. Business districts were located on Lake Street in Wayzata and Water Street in Excelsior. Mound City had two town centers—Busy Corners on Cooks Bay with shoreline hotels, a general store, and boat works, and Uptown to the north with liveries, a lumber yard, and a hardware store supporting the railroad extension by 1900. It eventually became an inland town center.

Citizens of each town filled multiple roles. Elmer Bardwell of Excelsior was the town mayor for three terms, a jeweler, and an undertaker. In Wayzata, Miles Dickey was president of the Cemetery Association, cofounder of the local Masonic Lodge, and founder of the library and Literary Club. Clarence "Curly" Koehler delivered groceries and was a volunteer firefighter in Mound. When the Great Depression began, Koehler became a charter member of the 29ers Club, a group promoting local lake businesses.

Farms and orchards thrived in the soil around the lake. In Excelsior, Alanson Latham cultivated grapes, and George Whipple found sweet sorghum more profitable to grow than wheat as customers preferred its taste to maple syrup. In Wayzata, Fred Braden originated an ever-bearing strawberry so popular it was demanded by European customers. The Excelsior and Minnetonka Fruit Growers' Associations organized cooperatives to improve marketing, especially raspberries, the most dependable fruit crop.

In 1880, James J. Hill's Aberdeen Angus cattle arrived on his Crystal Bay farm, Hillier. He added Jerseys and Ayrshires to fill his Hotel Lafayette needs and raised sheep, selling their fleece to North Star Woolen Mill in Minneapolis. At Maxwell Bay, Mabel Tuttle oversaw Little Orchard Farm, mothering her Jersey herd with attention to milk quality. Smithtown Bay's Boulder Bridge Farm raised prize-winning Guernseys, as owner George Dayton insisted his cows be milked by hand to maintain human contact. After World War II, large-acreage farms declined. Original owners were aging, and inherited acreage proved too costly to maintain. Land became more valuable as residential subdivisions.

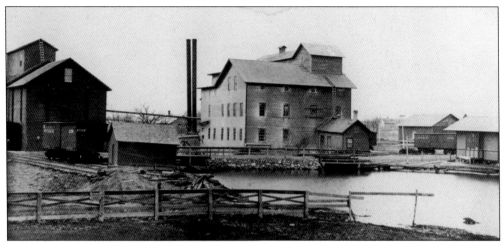

MINNETONKA MILL, MINNETONKA MILLS, C. 1883. A sawmill was constructed on Minnehaha Creek in 1853. After burning twice, a flour mill was built on the same site in 1869. The Minnetonka Mill Company purchased and enlarged the mill in the 1870s and began producing 300 to 400 barrels of flour daily, becoming among the first to make flour for export. It later became a gristmill and was dismantled in 1895. (ELMHS.)

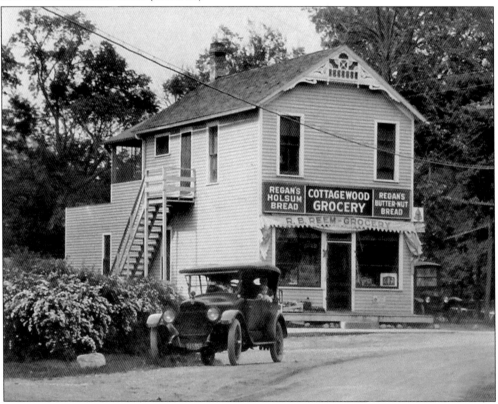

COTTAGEWOOD STORE, DEEPHAVEN, C. 1920. This store was built by Ralph and Stella Chapman in 1895 and catered to the summer trade of cottagers, campers, and guests of the Cottagewood and Keewaydin Hotels. It has seen many owners since its opening, but has always been the hub of Cottagewood. It remains one of the most historical structures in Deephaven. (CGS.)

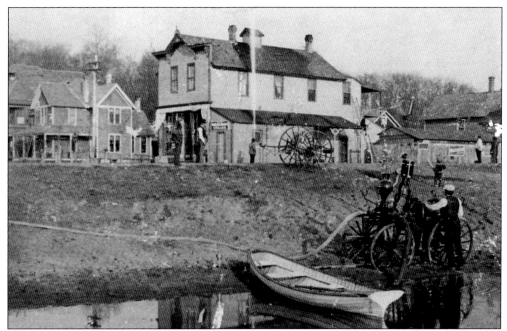

TESTING THE FIRST FIRE ENGINE, WAYZATA. The single-cylinder, gasoline-powered Waterous Engine is being tested as it draws water from the lake. Spraying into the air in front of the two-story Bushnell Building, testers sought a plume high enough to reach the top of the tallest building in town at the time. This engine was used in Wayzata from 1896 until 1910. (WZHS.)

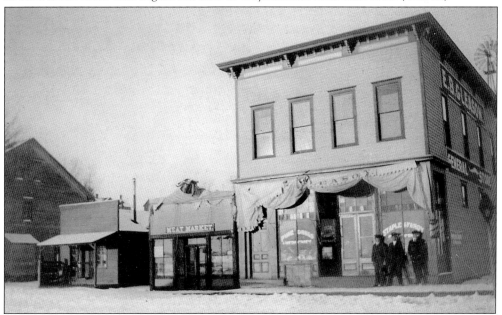

GLEASON STORE, WAYZATA. Eugene "Bonnie" Gleason opened his general store on the corner of Lake Street and Broadway in 1895. The ground floor sold merchandise, and the second level was used as a movie theater, doctors' offices, apartments, and a meeting space for the Odd Fellows. Gleason expanded his store in 1906, making it the largest in town. It was demolished in the 1960s. (WZHS.)

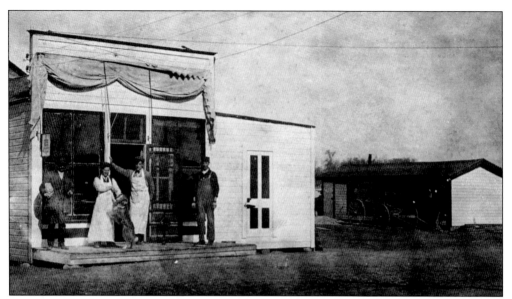

BROECKERT'S MEAT MARKET, MOUND, 1900. On the west side of Commerce Boulevard by Langdon Lake, Gustave Broeckert and Frank Weiland built their meat market. From left to right are Joe Laundry, Joe Winkel, August Glewwe, and Gustave Broeckert. The business was moved a block north and later operated by a second Broeckert generation. The building was demolished in the 1950s. (WTHS.)

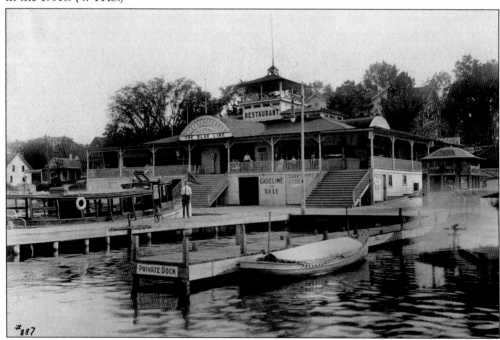

BLUE LINE PAVILION, EXCELSIOR. Located east of Water Street from 1904 until it burned in 1958, this café could serve 500 guests. It also rented boats and sold gas and bait. The boats were painted blue at the top, differentiating them from other boat rental shops. It was later used as a snack shop for the Excelsior Amusement Park. The small booth (right) still stands near its original location. (ELMHS.)

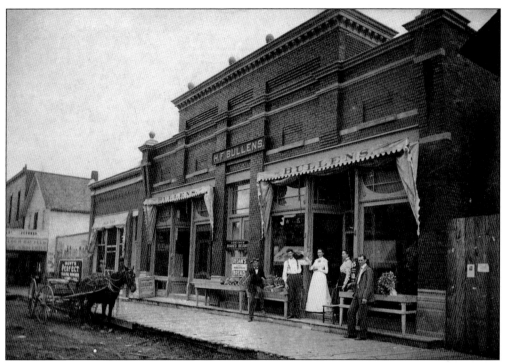

BULLEN'S GENERAL STORE, EXCELSIOR, C. 1902. Built almost entirely of brick in 1886 and still standing today, Bullen's Block is credited with stopping the 1902 fire on the east side of Water Street. The building was later split into three separate businesses. (ELMHS.)

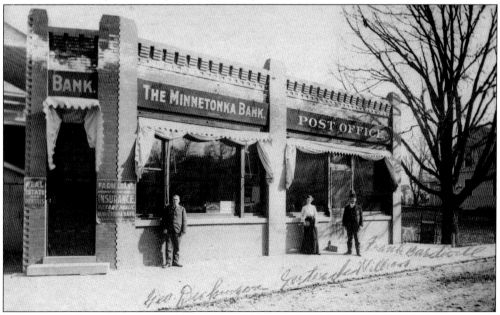

MINNETONKA BANK, EXCELSIOR, C. 1903. Built for the Minnetonka Bank by Charles Miller around 1899, a second story was added to the building in 1904. One side of the structure housed the post office until 1912, and the bank moved in 1917. Located at Second and Water Streets, the building appears much the same today as it did in 1904 and still houses a bank. (ELMHS.)

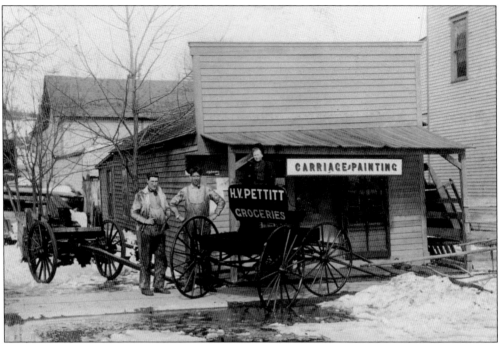

BOOMHOWER CARRIAGE PAINTING, WAYZATA. Herbert Westlake Boomhower's shop painted wagons, coaches, carriages, and sleighs, creating mobile works of art. Boomhower also painted the numbers on ships for the Navy during World War I, lettered boats at the Minnetonka Boat Works, and lettered and numbered the coats and hats for the Wayzata Fire Department. (WZHS.)

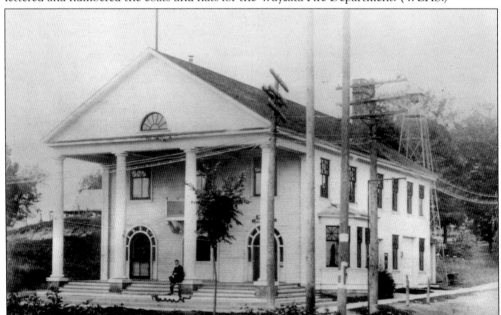

WAYZATA VILLAGE HALL. Built in 1904 at the corner of Lake Street and Manitoba Avenue for a reported cost of $3,977.75, the village hall housed the council chambers, jail, post office, library, and volunteer fire department's equipment. Miles Dickey, a Wayzata pioneer, set up the post office and library in this building, which burned in 1955. (WZHS.)

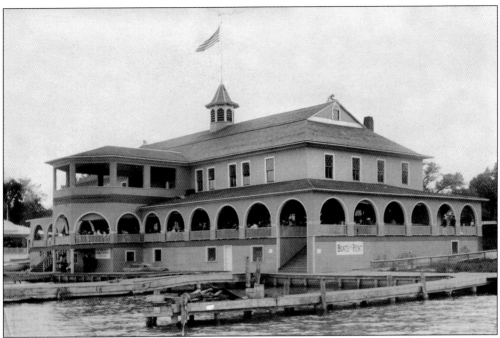

LAKE MINNETONKA CASINO, EXCELSIOR, 1904. Built in 1902 and catering to visitors seeking almost every form of amusement available at the time, the casino boasted a dance hall with full orchestra, a six-lane bowling alley (below), a roller-skating rink, billiard tables, and nonalcoholic refreshments. The casino was a fixture at the end of Water Street for 20 years, until its demolition in 1922. (Both, ELMHS.)

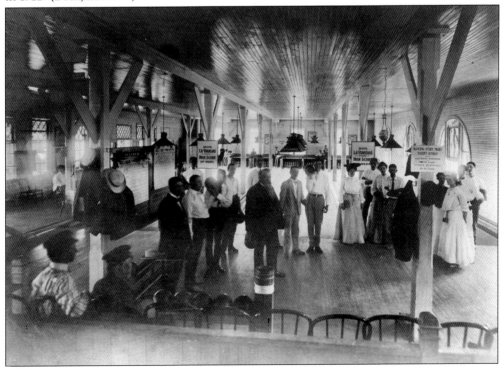

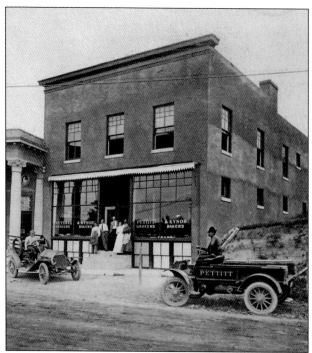

PETTITT & KYSOR GROCERY, WAYZATA. Harry Pettitt built a new grocery store next to the bank after his first business at Barry Avenue and Lake Street burned in 1910. Later, his brother-in-law George Kysor joined the business. They were popular for homemade baked goods, ice cream, and home delivery. Before telephone service, their horse and buggy made morning rounds, taking orders and delivering in time for dinner preparations. The building still stands. (WZHS.)

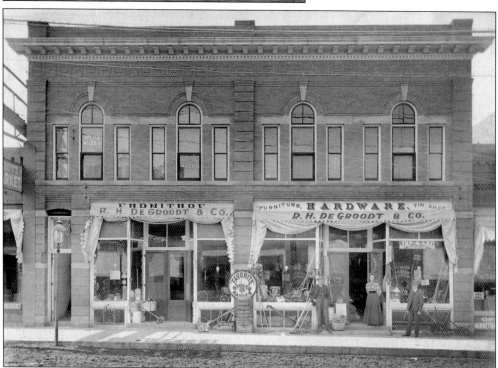

DEGROODT HARDWARE, EXCELSIOR. Built in 1900 as the Miller Building, this structure was a double store housing R.H. DeGroodt Hardware and Tin Shop. In 1932, the hardware store was on one side, and a millinery was on the other. Aldritt's Hardware bought the business in 1936. The building looks much the same today and stands at 234 Water Street. (ELMHS.)

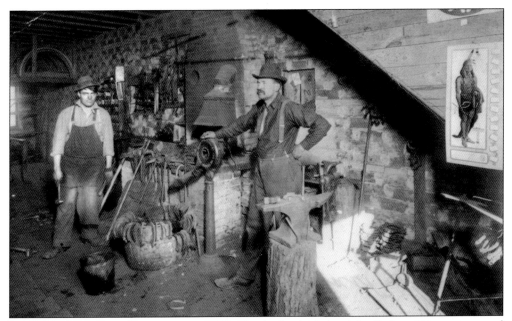

ICE BLACKSMITH SHOP, EXCELSIOR, C. 1910. Charles Ice (right), originally from Wayzata, opened his Excelsior blacksmith shop in 1910. The shop burned two years later, but was rebuilt and still stands at 278 Water Street. Ice remained a smith until 1917 and was one of the blacksmiths who provided shoes for the famous race horse Dan Patch, whose owner, Marion Savage, had a summer home in Excelsior. (ELMHS.)

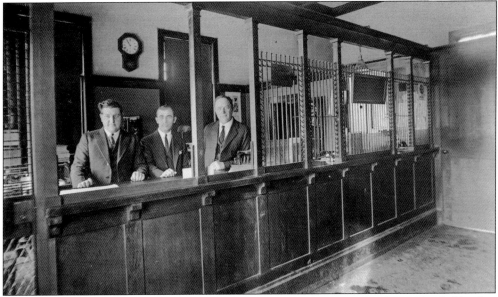

WAYZATA STATE BANK, 1924. Opening for business in 1909, this bank was funded by five businessmen including local boat builder Royal C. Moore. The full service management team consisted of, from left to right, vice presidents Alvin Frick and Walter Zastrow, and president Roswell Fairfield. The interior had three brass teller windows, a walk-in vault, and an office. Each teller had a buzzer that could alert Pettitt & Kysor's store next door if a robbery was in progress. The building is still standing. (WZHS.)

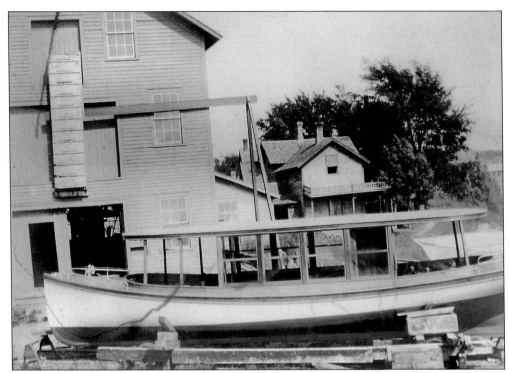

MOORE BOAT WORKS AND RAMALEY BOAT COMPANY, WAYZATA. Royal C. Moore and Gustavus Johnson partnered to form the Johnson-Moore Boat Works in 1880, located on the south side of Lake Street. They became well known for building boats every bit as good as Eastern builders. In 1888, Moore became sole proprietor, and the company became Moore Boat Works (above). In 1905, the Twin City Rapid Transit Company hired the company to design six streetcar boats. Moore's artistic and engineering abilities were reflected in the boats' graceful lines, the torpedo-style stern, and their "safe, quick and sturdy" reputation. In 1912, Moore sold his company, and the business was renamed Ramaley Boat Company. (Above, WZHS; below, HCL.)

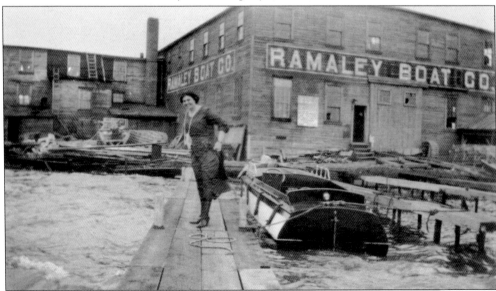

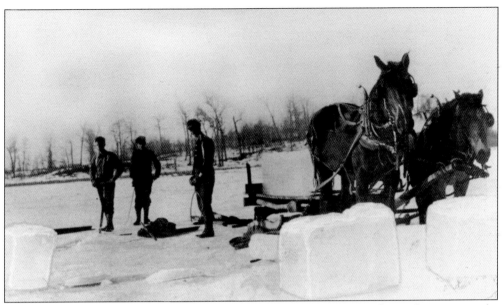

ICE HARVESTING. Ice harvesting and storage was a necessity prior to modern refrigeration and a thriving occupation on area bays. Lake preparation started with fall weed removal to ensure pure ice. Harvest began when the ice was 14 to 24 inches thick, per customer requests. A checkerboard design was etched onto the ice, and blocks were cut using long-handled chisels and saws. Difficult and hazardous labor, local newspapers told stories about "daring young fellows" on the ice, jumping from block to block and sometimes landing in icy waters. Here, blocks are loaded onto a horse-drawn wagon on Maxwell Bay (above) and delivered to nearby icehouses for storage or the train for delivery into the city (below). Each community kept at least one ice storage house throughout the summer, using hay and sawdust as insulation between the cakes. Customers included the Lafayette Club and the Stubbs Bay Creamery. (Above, HHM; below, WZHS.)

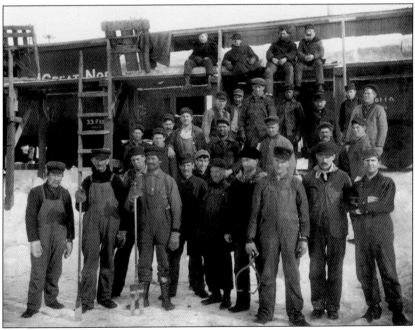

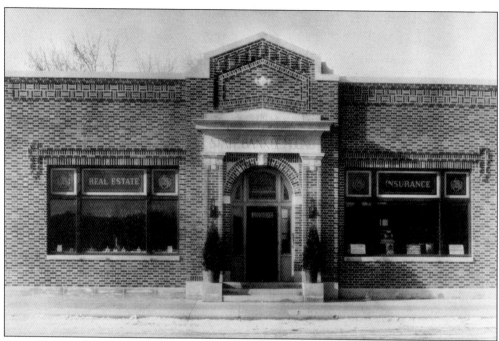

STATE BANK OF MOUND. In 1909, Emil Chladek and his father-in-law, Mathias Hegerle, cofounded the first bank in town on the west side of Commerce Boulevard. In the early years, Chladek was president and cashier and was assisted by his wife, Anna, and local Methodist minister Reverend Morehouse. William Koehler (below right) and Frank Groschen bought the business in 1913, and Koehler assumed the role of president until he retired in 1956. Koehler, formerly the town's lumberyard owner, humorously claimed that his primary interest in buying the bank was because he was envious of the banker's hours. The original building still remains and has housed various businesses over the years. (Above, TR; below, WTHS.)

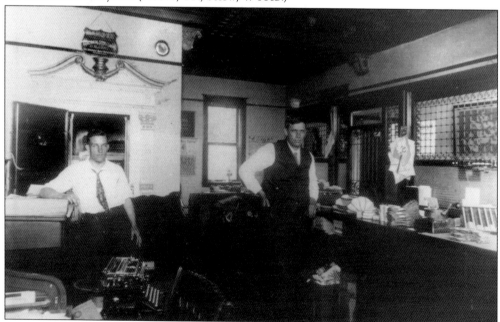

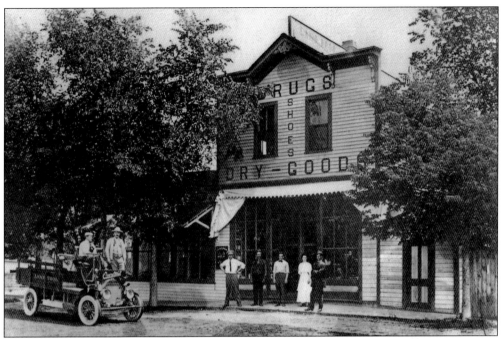

LAMB BROTHERS DRY GOODS & GROCERY, WAYZATA. This building began life at the foot of Broadway Avenue around 1878 as a saloon owned by George Reid. When Wayzata became a dry village in 1884, Reid sold the building to William Bushnell, who established a general store that also housed the post office. Bushnell sold to brothers Lorin and Charles Lamb in 1906, and the business prospered, selling everything imaginable. Below is the interior of the store in 1911 with Lorin standing at right and Charles behind the counter. In 1925, the Lambs sold the store to Hart DuPrey, who removed the second floor and opened the iconic Hart's Café. (Both, WZHS.)

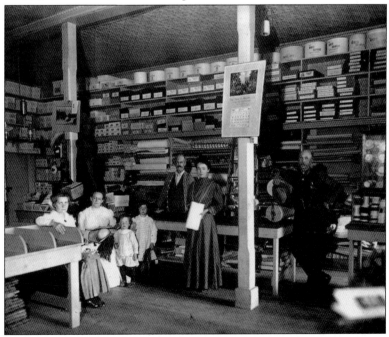

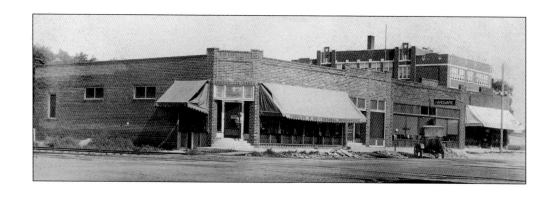

KOEHLER GROCERY STORE, MOUND. Edward Koehler, whose parents moved to Minnetrista from Illinois in the 1860s, opened his grocery store in 1910. Pictured above in 1917, it was located on the west side of Commerce Boulevard near the railroad tracks. Fire destroyed the first building in 1924, and Koehler rebuilt. By 1929, his son-in-law Fred Clark owned the business, and it became an IGA franchise. The store interior, seen below around 1938, was merchandised by longtime employee Cal Inman, who featured produce at the windows to attract customers. Butcher Charlie Anderson worked in the rear. At the north end of the store, a second door led customers into the post office, where Koehler's brother William was acting postmaster. When Clark sold to Super Valu, the market moved, and the building remained home to various enterprises until it was demolished in 2012. (Both, WTHS.)

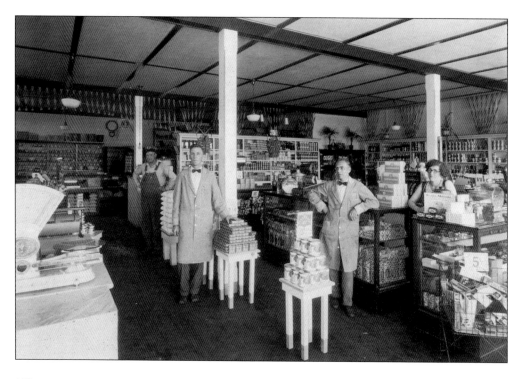

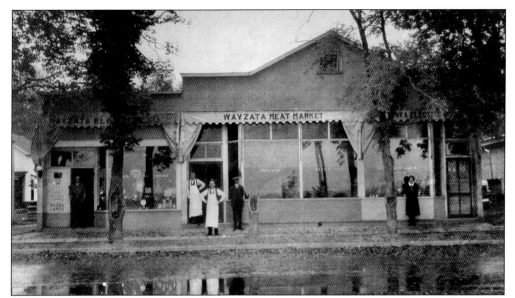

Wayzata Meat Market. Jarvis Dougherty opened the town meat market in 1911 and sold it to James Dobson in 1919. At that time, butcher shops began to expand their offerings, striving to be a one-stop-shop for customers, carrying canned goods and breakfast cereals. Children were tempted by bubble gum and penny candy on the counter. (WZHS.)

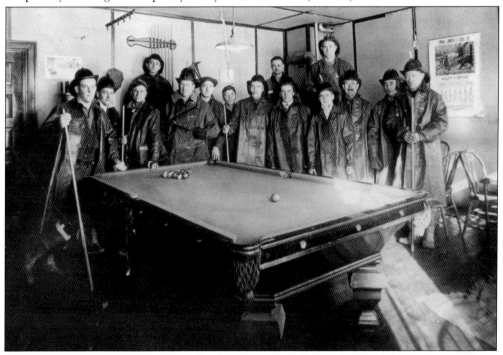

Wayzata Fire Department. In 1924, the department proudly stands around their newest purchase, a $125 pool table. A month prior to this photograph, chief Reed Keesling requested from the village council a space to be used as a recreation area for the volunteer firefighters. The council gave them a small room in the village hall and allowed them to use the pool table from noon until midnight. (WZHS.)

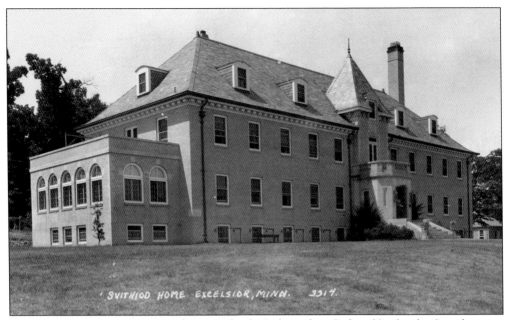

SVITHIOD HOME, SHOREWOOD. Built in 1927 by the Independent Order of Svithiod, a Scandinavian heritage organization, this 42-room house was home to ambulatory seniors who wished to retire in a resort setting. Each resident occupied a small room and shared the cooking, cleaning, and gardening. On Sundays, the house served chicken dinners to the public. It closed in the late 1950s and was demolished in 2004. (ELMHS.)

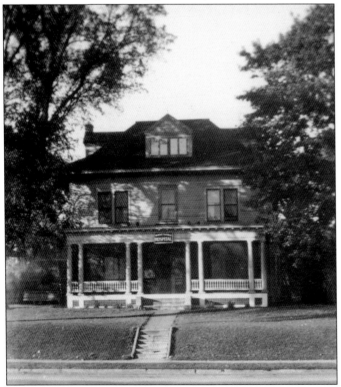

MINNETONKA HOSPITAL, WAYZATA, C. 1929. Founded in 1928 by Dr. Carl Martinson of Wayzata and Dr. Edward Mitchell of Mound, the hospital was housed in this building from 1928 to 1964. Doctors performed surgeries, set bones, sutured wounds, and delivered over 1,500 babies. In addition to medical services, it was known for its home-cooked meals, rumored to be among the best in the area. (WZHS.)

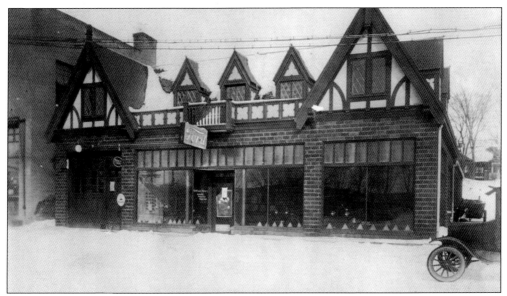

RETTINGER MOTOR COMPANY, LAKE STREET, WAYZATA. Built in 1927 by Sam Rettinger of Long Lake, this business featured Tudor Revival–style architecture with a stucco and brick finish, unusual for commercial designs at the time. With offices in the front and the garage in the rear, Rettinger's sold Model Ts as well as Ford tractors. Upstairs was a gun range for target practice using sandbags. The building burned in 1952. (WZHS.)

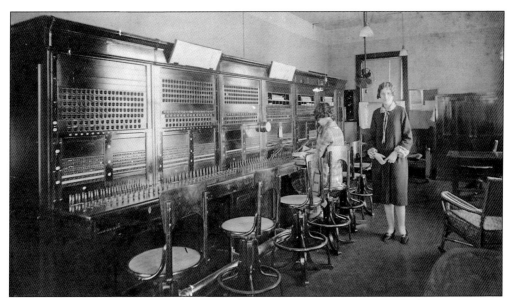

WAYZATA TELEPHONE COMPANY, 1926. In 1897, Wayzata granted a franchise to Northwestern Telephone Exchange to wire the town for telephone and telegraph. The telephone building on Barry Avenue housed the switchboard on its second floor. Operators answered with the familiar phrase "Number please?" and responded to emergency calls. (WZHS.)

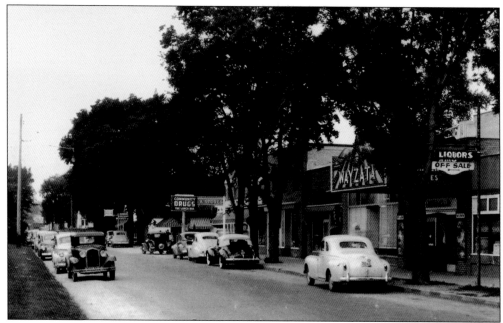

WAYZATA MOVIE THEATER, LAKE STREET. Owned by Lyle Carisch and Raymond Lee, the theater opened in 1932 with an Art Deco design and multicolored motif. Admission was 35¢ for adults and 10¢ for children. Until concessions were offered in the 1940s, customers could bring snacks. The theater's early air-conditioning system of water misted from vents was popular with customers but caused a slippery lobby floor. The business closed in 1986, and a reproduction of the marquee remains. (WZHS.)

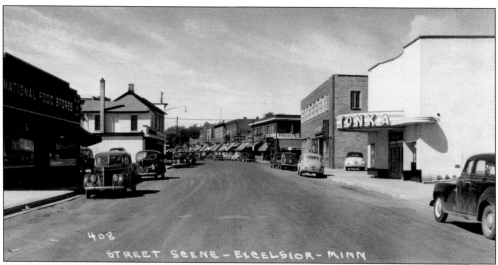

WATER STREET, EXCELSIOR, 1948. This view of Water Street looking southwest includes the Tonka Theater (right). It was built in 1945 on the same spot that its five-year-old predecessor had occupied before burning to the ground. The new 500-seat fireproof building had an interior decor that featured a yachting and steamboat theme. The Excelsior Dock Cinema operates three screens in the building today. (ELMHS.)

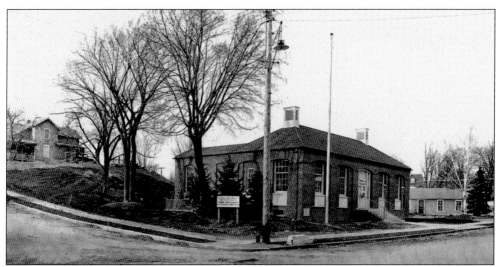

WAYZATA POST OFFICE. The first post office building was built in 1942 as a WPA project following World War II, but mail delivery in Wayzata dates to 1854. Until the early 1900s, the post office was found in a local hotel or general store. Its first permanent home came in 1904, when the original village hall was built. (WZHS.)

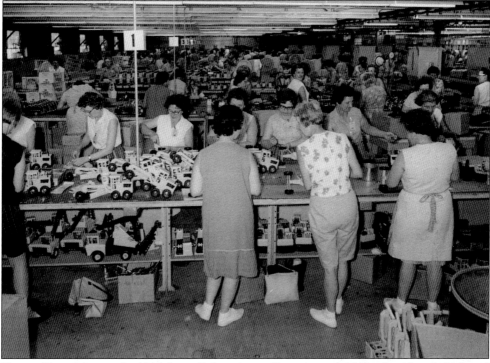

TONKA TOYS, MOUND. In 1946, Lynn Baker, Avery Crounse, and Al Tesch cofounded Mound Metalcraft, making household products. In 1947, Ed Streater of Spring Park sold his wooden toy plans to the trio and changed the company's future. Switching to the production of sturdy metal toys made near the shores of Lake Minnetonka, the company became Tonka Toys in 1955. The plant closed in 1983 when manufacturing moved to Texas and Mexico. The block-long complex along Shoreline Drive still stands today. (WTHS.)

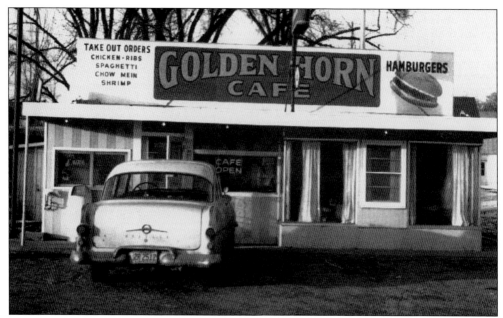

THE GOLDEN HORN CAFÉ, SPRING PARK. Andrew and Olga Kitchar built the Horn in the 1950s on County Road 15, across from Spring Park Bay. The café was open 24 hours, serving breakfast and lunch to locals, late dinners to the nightclub crowd, and hosting break time for the Spring Park policemen. After a series of owners, it closed in 1978 and was demolished in 1983. (TR.)

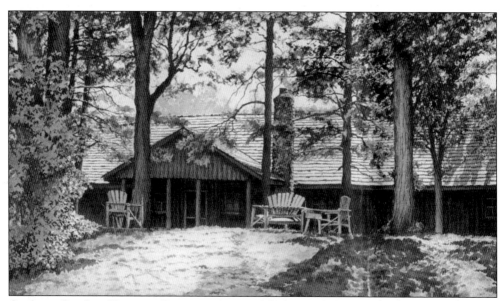

ORIGINAL OLD LOG THEATER, GREENWOOD. One of the longest continuously operating professional theaters in the country, the Old Log started in 1940 as a summer stock theater in the converted log stable shown here in a painting by Francis R. Meisch. By 1960, a new theater twice as large was built, operating year round and featuring a full-service restaurant. Owned and operated by the Don Stolz family for almost 70 years, the Old Log continues today under new ownership. (ELMHS.)

PETER GIDEON. Gideon arrived in 1853, and over the next 11 years planted 350 apple trees, attempting to develop the first Minnesota winter hardy apple. He succeeded in 1868 with the Wealthy, named after his wife and still grown today. Superintendent of the Minnesota Experimental Fruit Farm, Gideon was known as the "father of fruit breeding on the prairies" and an early advocate of abolition, prohibition, women's suffrage, and the rights of Indians. (ELMHS.)

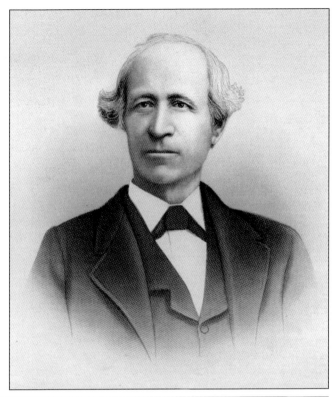

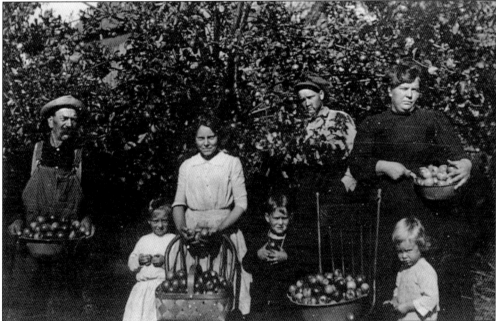

APPLE HARVEST. At the August Keckhafer farm along Dutch Lake in Mound, everyone in the family helped with the apple harvest at summer's end. Without refrigeration in 1905, the crop was kept fresh during the winter months by individually wrapping each apple and storing them in the cellar. Neighbors shared their yield or sold surplus at the local general store. (WTHS.)

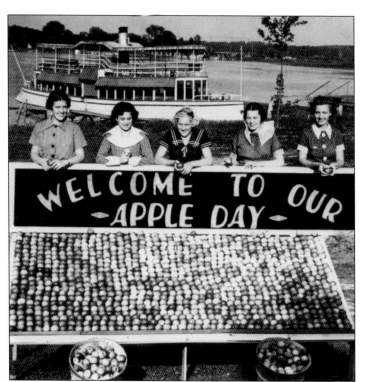

FIRST APPLE DAY CELEBRATION, EXCELSIOR, 1935. By 1935, the Excelsior area was filled with apple orchards and celebrated the harvest with Apple Day. For six years, the event drew thousands and featured apple-themed decorations, games, prizes, concerts, dances, a doll-buggy parade and the crowning of an Apple Queen. Here, queen and court stand behind a display of fresh apples. Apple Day resumed in 1985 and is still celebrated today. (ELMHS.)

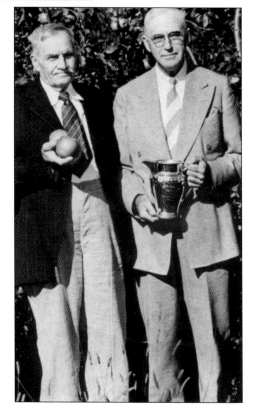

CHARLES HARALSON, 1939. Fruit breeder and horticulturist Charles Haralson (left), pictured here with John Wilson, was a Deephaven resident credited with developing the Haralson apple in 1923; the variety is still popular today. He served as the superintendent of the University of Minnesota Fruit Breeding Farm at Zumbra Heights for 18 years and is praised for developing winter hardy fruit varieties, including the Latham raspberry. (ELMHS.)

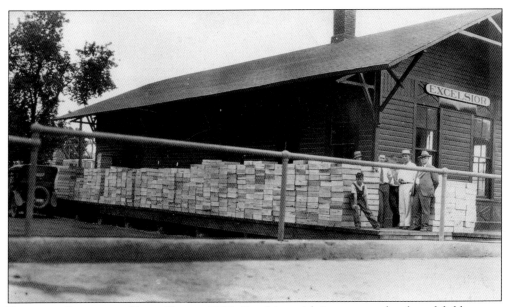

Excelsior Depot and Berry Boxes, 1929. Excelsior, with its many orchards and fields, was a major supplier of fruit. The Excelsior Fruit Growers' Association was organized in 1900, and in 1929, shipped 70 carloads of berries by rail as far west as the Dakotas, with almost $300,000 in total sales. It disbanded in 1969, when few local growers were active. (ELMHS.)

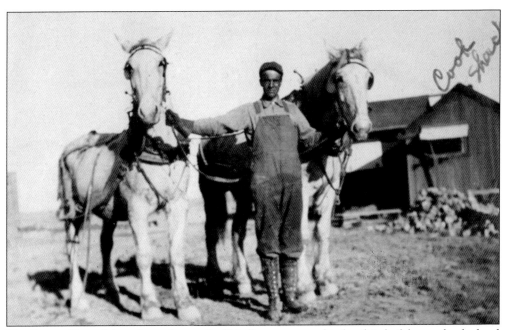

The Family Team. Mound-area farmer Paul Hoffman prepares his family's draft horses for the hard work day. As on most farms, this team was the backbone of the workforce in 1900. Considered very important animals, they were depended upon for plowing, planting, and harvesting, plus hauling and transportation. (WTHS.)

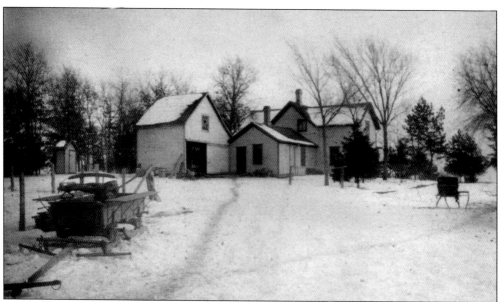

SPRUCE GROVE FARM, PLYMOUTH. Alexander and Mary Winnen Frick both had long family histories in the Lake Minnetonka area. Their farm was located at the corner of Vicksburg Lane and County Road 15, and they sold produce from a booth at the Central Market in Minneapolis. The farm was demolished, and the new Wayzata High School was built on the site in 1961. (WZHS.)

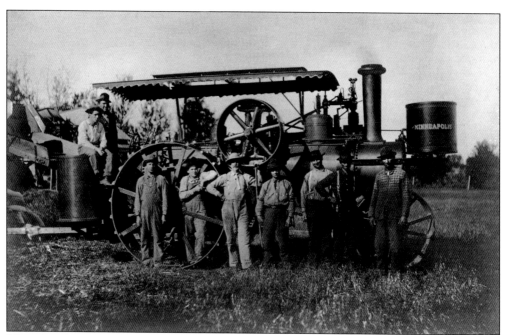

MACHINE FARMING. In the manually intensive world of farming around Lake Minnetonka, one man could hand reap about a quarter of an acre of wheat in a day. By 1890, these Minnetrista farmers used machines, allowing two men and two horses to cut, rake, and bind 20 acres of wheat per day. Neighbors shared the cost of machine rental or purchase, supporting one another by harvesting acreage together. (WTHS.)

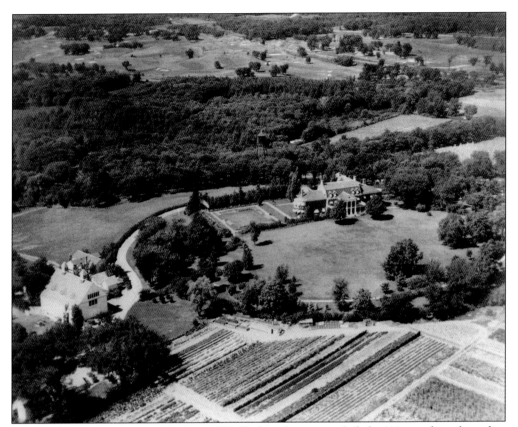

HIGHCROFT FARM, WAYZATA. Built in 1895, Highcroft estate included a 111-acre dairy farm that employed 35 herdsmen for the dairy barns. By 1930, the Heffelfinger's Guernsey herd ranked among the highest producing in the country, winning prizes at state fairs and national competitions. The family sold the farm and herd after 1942. (WZHS.)

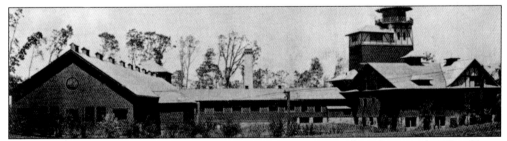

WOODEND FARM, MINNETRISTA, 1905. Albert Loring's 1,000-acre dairy farm on the West Upper Lake was in high production from 1901 through 1932. Among several gentlemen farmers around Lake Minnetonka, Loring created a model of modern farming focusing on barn ventilation and cleanliness. His Guernseys and Holsteins were considered some of the best in the state, repeatedly breaking records for butterfat production. (ELMHS.)

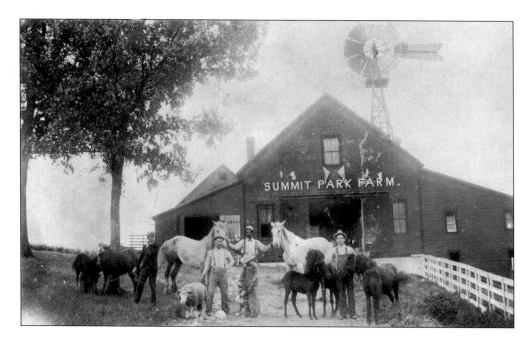

SUMMIT PARK BARN AND FARMHOUSE, WAYZATA. By the mid-1950s, Wayzata had five dairy farms remaining, including the Summit Park Farm, named for a stop on the Luce Line Railroad. The 360-acre farm was purchased by Samuel H. Bowman Sr. in 1909. Bowman's approach to dairy farming was to arrange for local peddlers to bottle and deliver the milk his herd produced. From 1935 until 1952, the farm was leased by the Sween Brothers' Dairy, and at its largest it had 60 milk cows, a creamery, and over 1,000 Leghorn laying hens. By 1956, the Bowman family was ready to sell and felt that the "larger interest of the community was to maintain the open space that the farm provided." Rather than a housing subdivision, the land became the Wayzata Golf and Hunt Club, today standing as Wayzata Country Club. (Both, WZHS.)

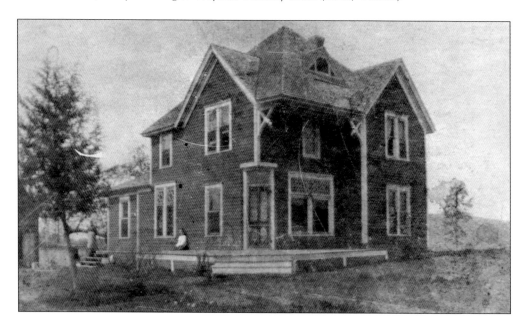

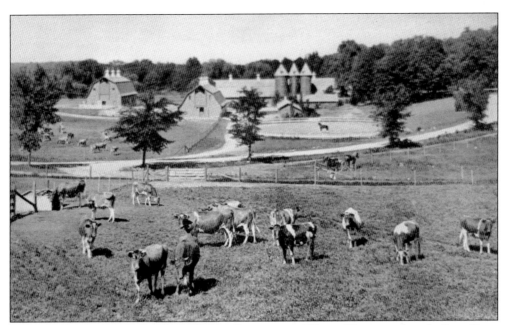

BOULDER BRIDGE FARM AND DAIRY BARN, SHOREWOOD. Edmund Longyear bought Rose Farm near Smithtown Bay in 1906 for use as a summer residence. In 1907, he completed a 10,000-square-foot house and boathouse and dredged the lagoon, adding a fieldstone bridge. George and Grace Dayton became the owners in 1926, changing the estate name to Boulder Bridge after the existing bridge across the lagoon. Dayton expanded the farm to 800 acres and raised 200 Guernseys, 70 Belgian horses, and other livestock, plus all the feed. His breeding programs won international accolades, and his animals were national and international champions. The farm was self sustaining, supplying milk and cream to the Dayton's department store tearooms. The dairy barn is pictured below around 1935. In 1950, the farm was auctioned off; it was subdivided in the 1980s, and the house with four acres remains today. (Both, HHM.)

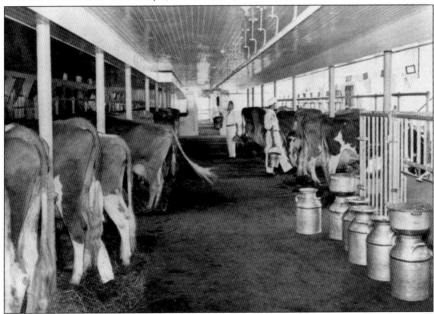

BIBLIOGRAPHY

Bergmann, Richards *The Early Background of Minnetonka Beach.* Minneapolis, MN: Hennepin County Historical Society, 1991.

Excelsior–Lake Minnetonka Historical Society. *Walking the Trails of History.* Excelsior, MN: Excelsior–Lake Minnetonka Historical Society, 2002.

Gimmestad, Melvin. *Historical Backgrounds of Mound, Minnesota.* St. Paul, MN: Macalester College, 1964.

Hallberg, Jane King. *Minnehaha Creek.* Minneapolis, MN: Cityscapes Publishing, 1995.

Johnson, Frederick L. *The Big Water.* Deephaven, MN: Deep Haven Books, 2012.

Larson, Paul Clifford. *A Place at the Lake.* Afton, MN: Afton Historical Society, 1998.

Magnuson, Jeff. *Historical Tour of the Westonka Area, Year 2012.* Westonka, MN: Westonka Historical Society, 2011.

McGinnis, Scott D. *A Directory of Old Boats, Lake Minnetonka's Historic Steamboats, Sailboats and Launches.* Chaska, MN: Self-published, 2010.

———. *Excelsior's Waterfront: The History of the Excelsior Commons and Excelsior Docks.* Chaska, MN: Self-published, 2008.

Meyer, Ellen Wilson. *Happenings Around Lake Minnetonka. The First 100 Years, 1853–1953.* Wayzata, MN: Self-published, 1983.

———. *Lake Minnetonka's Historic Hotels.* Excelsior, MN: Excelsior–Lake Minnetonka Historical Society, 1997.

Minnetonka Yacht Club. *Minnetonka Yacht Club Centennial 1882–1982.* Deephaven, MN: Minnetonka Yacht Club Sailing School, 1982.

Myers, Pamela J. *Classroom Voices 1850s–1950s: Student Memories of Grade Schools and Mound Consolidated High School, District #85.* Minneapolis, MN: Syren Book Company, 2009.

Rockvam, Tom. *The Andrew Sisters.* Mound, MN: Self-published, 2011.

Westonka Historical Society. *Mound, One Hundred Years, A monthly look into history.* Westonka, MN: Westonka Historical Society, 2012.

ABOUT THE ORGANIZATIONS

EXCELSIOR–LAKE MINNETONKA HISTORICAL SOCIETY. Founded in 1972, the society collects the history of Excelsior, Greenwood, Shorewood, and Tonka Bay, as well as parts of Deephaven and Orono. Its mission is to preserve, document, and classify the physical history of the Lake Minnetonka area; to provide a means by which everyone can share in the history of the lake area; and stimulate interest in the cultural heritage of the area. The society's archives and museum are free and open to the public, and it has published a number of books about Lake Minnetonka history. The society also presents programs on topics of local historical interest. For more information: www.elmhs.org, info@elmhs.org, 952-221-4766.

WAYZATA HISTORICAL SOCIETY. The society was founded in 1982 to document, preserve, and share the history of Wayzata and surrounding Lake Minnetonka communities. It operates the Depot Museum from May through December, the Garden Railroad from May through October (weather permitting), and a research archives year-round, with local history books available for purchase. Additionally, the *Telegraph* newsletter is published four times each year, and programs about local history are presented to the public quarterly. As topics of historical interest arise, a special event may be planned for the community. For more information: www.wayzatahistoricalsociety.org, info@wayzatahistoricalsociety.org, 952-473-3631.

WESTONKA HISTORICAL SOCIETY AND HISTORY MUSEUM. The society, founded in 1966, compiles the history of Minnetrista, Mound, Spring Park, and the portions of Orono and Independence within the Westonka School District. It is committed to preserving records, gathering artifacts, and making the history of the Westonka area accessible to all. The society has a research archive with an extensive postcard collection, a gift shop with numerous books by local authors, and a museum open to the public including a large Tonka Toys exhibit. Events are hosted monthly, private museum tours are available by appointment, and a quarterly newsletter is offered for members. For more information: www.westonkahistoricalsociety.org.

ADDITIONAL LAKE MINNETONKA HISTORICAL RESOURCES:
Deephaven Historical Society, www.cityofdeephaven.org
Minnesota Streetcar Museum, www.trolleyride.org
Minnetonka Historical Society, www.minnetonka-history.org
Museum of Lake Minnetonka, www.steamboatminnehaha.org
Western Hennepin County Pioneer Association, www.whcpa-museum.org

DISCOVER THOUSANDS OF LOCAL HISTORY BOOKS FEATURING MILLIONS OF VINTAGE IMAGES

Arcadia Publishing, the leading local history publisher in the United States, is committed to making history accessible and meaningful through publishing books that celebrate and preserve the heritage of America's people and places.

Find more books like this at
www.arcadiapublishing.com

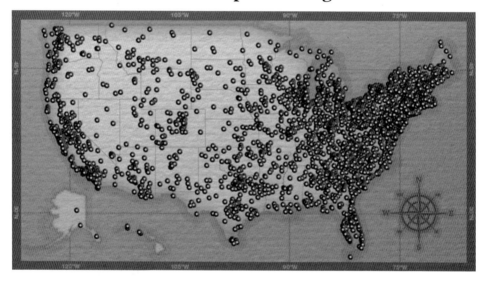

Search for your hometown history, your old stomping grounds, and even your favorite sports team.

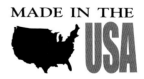